"In her latest book, *Family Therapy and the Treatment of Substance Use Disorders*, Dr. Melody Bacon offers an innovative approach to a problem that has plagued individuals, families, and societies for millennia. By outlining the history of substance use and the efforts taken in the US to combat the devastating results of misuse, she provides the context for introducing her Family Matters Program. This integration of Bowen Family Systems Theory with the 12-step program of Alcoholics Anonymous is a much-needed addition to our tools to help families find healing and freedom from addiction."

*Rigo Brueck, PhD, Clinical Director, Covenant Hills Treatment Centers, Inc.*

"Dr. Bacon's book *Family Therapy and the Treatment of Substance Use Disorders* offers fresh hope and practical guidance for working with one of the most challenging populations in mental health. Much needed, this book awakens even experienced clinicians to new possibilities for treatment and recovery."

*Diane R. Gehart, PhD, author of Mastering Competencies in Family Therapy and Professor, California State University, Northridge*

"Dr. Bacon's lively inquiry, compassionate nature, and practical wisdom make this book a pleasure to read. Useful for those who are new to the field as well as more experienced practitioners, this book makes an important contribution to the available literature on the treatment of substance use disorders. The balance of context, real-life stories, and expert reflection make this book a vibrant learning experience for the reader. Dr. Bacon's Family Matters Program is an emerging and promising addiction treatment paradigm. As I read this book, I was impressed with how effortlessly Dr. Bacon weaves together themes of family therapy, psychodynamic insight, and behavioral change. In these pages you will find an optimistic voice describing the avenues for growth that are within reach for those with substance use disorders as well as their families."

*Sean Sterling, PhD, ABPP, Department Chair, Applied Clinical Psychology Program, The Chicago School of Professional Psychology*

# FAMILY THERAPY AND THE TREATMENT OF SUBSTANCE USE DISORDERS

This accessible guide offers a much-needed integration of family therapy into the treatment of substance use disorders. By proposing a means by which family therapy can be moved to the forefront of addiction treatment, it places the family perspective at the center of its approach and provides a multifaceted alternative to the prevalent individual-focused model.

Drawing from Bowen Family Systems Theory and the principles of the 12-step program, the book presents a model of integration that addresses the needs of families struggling with addiction. Illustrated with discussion questions and case narratives of former addicts, the text guides both practitioners and families towards a goal of creating an environment that supports recovery. Offering an overview of the history and current models of addiction treatment, chapters also outline a 6-week Family Matters Program, with accompanying treatment interventions and case studies. The book concludes with an examination of how this program can be implemented by practitioners in a variety of clinical settings.

*Family Therapy and the Treatment of Substance Use Disorders* is essential reading for anyone with an interest in understanding the diverse ways in which addiction affects families. It will be particularly relevant to students of family therapy, but clinicians who work across the fields of substance abuse treatment or family counseling will also benefit from reading this book.

**Melody Bacon, PhD,** is a professor at The Chicago School of Professional Psychology in the Marriage and Family Therapy department and a member of the American Association of Marriage and Family Therapy (AAMFT). Dr. Bacon is a clinical psychologist specializing in relational issues and has been in practice for over 20 years.

# FAMILY THERAPY AND THE TREATMENT OF SUBSTANCE USE DISORDERS

## The Family Matters Model

*Melody Bacon*

Routledge
Taylor & Francis Group
NEW YORK AND LONDON

First published 2019
by Routledge
52 Vanderbilt Avenue, New York, NY 10017

and by Routledge
2 Park Square, Milton Park, Abingdon, Oxon, OX14 4RN

*Routledge is an imprint of the Taylor & Francis Group, an informa business*



*Library of Congress Cataloging-in-Publication Data*
A catalog record for this title has been requested

ISBN: 978-1-138-72470-9 (hbk)
ISBN: 978-1-138-72477-8 (pbk)
ISBN: 978-1-315-19225-3 (ebk)

Typeset in Joanna
by Swales & Willis, Exeter, Devon, UK

# CONTENTS

# INTRODUCTION

> The world we see that seems so insane is the result of a belief system that is not working. To perceive the world differently, we must be willing to change our belief system, let the past slip away, expand our sense of now, and dissolve the fear in our minds.
>
> William James

Every problem of human experience is, in some ways, a relationship problem. As a psychologist in training at a behavioral medicine unit, I conducted psychotherapy groups for individuals struggling with a variety of diagnoses – depression, bipolar disorder, schizophrenia, eating disorders, chemical dependency. Despite the differences in diagnosis, what the patients shared in common was the pain and distress these disorders brought to their primary relationships.

Nowhere is this more apparent than in the lives of those struggling with substance abuse. The devastation of this disease – lost jobs, broken relationships, trips to the emergency room, time spent acquiring and using their drug of choice – affects not only the addict or alcoholic but the lives of their family and friends. As Beverly Conyers, a family member of an addict, describes:

> For almost every addict who's mired in this terrible disease, others – a mother or father, a child or spouse, an aunt or uncles or grandparents, a brother or sister – are suffering too. Families are the hidden victims of addiction, enduring enormous levels of stress and pain. They suffer sleepless nights, deep anxiety, and physical exhaustion brought on by worry and desperation.
>
> (Conyers, 2009, p. 10)

It is ironic, then, that due to the effect of addiction on the brain, the alcoholic or addict is unable to accurately assess the negative impact of substance abuse on themselves or others. In addition, since pain is the primary motivator of change, and because addicts and alcoholics have found something – their drug of choice – to anesthetize their pain, it is the family members who experience the most pain over their loved one's addiction. As a result, it falls to motivated and influential individuals to make the necessary changes in the family system to support the recovery of the addict or alcoholic and to improve their own lives in the process.

This is the approach that is advocated in the Treatment Improvement Protocol (TIP) published by SAMHSA (Substance Abuse and Mental Health Services Administration) on Family Therapy and Substance Abuse (2004):

> The family has a central role to play in the treatment of any health problem, including substance abuse. Family work has become a strong and continuing theme of many treatment approaches (Kaufmann and Kaufman 1992a; McCrady and Epstein 1996), but family therapy is not used to its greatest capacity in substance abuse treatment. A primary challenge remains to broaden the substance abuse treatment focus from the individual to the family.
>
> (p. 1)

Marriage and family therapists and other clinicians who work within the context of the family system are in a unique position to address this challenge. Current treatment approaches, while necessary, fall short of addressing the issues of the relational and emotional environment of the addict or alcoholic, the family system. One reason for this is that training in family systems is often cursory and the dominant narrative to the field of psychotherapy holds the individual as pre-eminent and the family system as inconsequential, particularly in working with adults. As a result, the pre-licensed psychotherapist is unlikely to find support for the use of a family systems approach in the majority of substance abuse treatment programs.

If outcomes for substance abuse treatment were stronger, one might argue that there is no need to include family systems therapy. But reported rates of recovery remain at an estimated 40%–60%, and sobriety after treatment is tenuous (NIDA, 2012, p. 12). Though eventually most, though not all, individuals will experience lasting recovery, usually this occurs after multiple relapses and treatment episodes. The emotional rollercoaster experience of family members who must watch this process is painful and challenging. The devastation of addiction and alcoholism cuts a wide swath not only through the lives of those struggling with substance abuse but equally those who love them. The dreaded midnight phone call either from the addict out on another run or the police officer bearing bad news is the ultimate source of anxiety and countless sleepless nights.

As the authors of the SAMHSA TIP 39 (2004) suggest, it is time to integrate the approach of family systems therapy with substance abuse treatment (p. 2). Each of these fields can offer something to the treatment of the addict/alcoholic and the family system as a whole. This represents an integrated and comprehensive approach to addiction treatment that will benefit all concerned.

Though the addict or alcoholic is an easy target for blame, from a family systems view, this individual, rather than being the cause of the problem, is the symptom bearer of the family as a whole. Given this assumption, it stands to reason that substance abuse treatment should include family therapy since this would facilitate change in the emotional and relational environment.

In keeping with this assumption, and the recommendations of the SAMHSA task force, this book offers a way to move the field of psychotherapy in this direction by applying the basic principles of Bowen Family Systems Theory to the treatment of substance abuse. Chapter 1 sets the stage with an exploration of substance abuse within the historical context of human experience. This provides the reader with an understanding of the power and intransigence of substance use and abuse in human culture. Chapters 2 and 3 present an overview of the history of addiction treatment in the United States and an overview of the philosophy and principles of Alcoholics Anonymous and the 12-step movement, respectively. Taken together, these three chapters set the backdrop for understanding the current challenges and opportunities of substance abuse treatment.

Chapter 4 provides a review of the current standard treatment models of alcoholism and addiction treatment in the United States and in Chapter 5 readers will find an overview of research conducted on family therapy and substance abuse treatment. The heart of the book is presented in Chapter 6 which offers an in-depth presentation of the Family Matters Program, a model of addiction treatment based on the ideas of Bowen Family Systems Theory and the program of Alcoholics Anonymous. Finally, Chapter 7 concludes this book with an examination of how the Family Matters Program can be implemented by practitioners in a variety of clinical settings.

Each chapter is followed by a brief narrative of an individual's experience of alcoholism and/or addiction. These are the stories of addicts and alcoholics in recovery who volunteered to share their experiences so that those who read this book can gain greater insight and understanding into the lived experience of addiction. Discussion questions are included at the end of each chapter to assist in exploring the ideas presented.

As the authors of SAMHSA TIP 39 explain:

> Clients benefit in several ways from integrated family therapy and substance abuse treatment. These benefits include positive treatment outcomes, increased likelihood of the client's ongoing recovery, increased help for the family's recovery, and the reduction of the impact of substance abuse on different generations in the family. The benefits for the treatment professionals include reduced resistance from clients, more flexibility in treatment planning and in treatment approach, increased skill set, and improved treatment outcomes.
>
> (p. 12)

Students who study family systems theory, and clinicians who work from a family systems model, have the opportunity to stand at the vanguard of substance abuse treatment and the call for an integrative approach. This book represents one model of how this approach can be implemented; it is hoped that the ideas explored within these pages will stimulate others to venture forth in this direction, to better serve addicts, alcoholics and the families who love them.

# 1

# THE ENTWINED HISTORY OF HUMAN CULTURE AND MOOD-ALTERING SUBSTANCES

> First you take a drink, then the drink takes a drink, then the drink takes you.
>
> F. Scott Fitzgerald

> The mouth of a perfectly contented man is filled with beer.
>
> Ancient Egyptian proverb

When it comes to understanding, context makes a big difference. Imagine looking at a close-up photograph of a young woman, standing in front of the Eiffel Tower. You might assume she was in Paris, France. Now imagine viewing this same photograph shot from further away; you might see that she is actually in Las Vegas, Nevada, standing in front of the Paris Las Vegas hotel. Without being able to view the full context of the scene, you might have drawn the wrong conclusion. The same can be said for understanding the phenomenon of addiction; you need the full context in order to draw accurate conclusions. This chapter will review the history of alcohol and other mood-altering substances as a context for the treatment of substance use disorders.

History provides the context for much of human experience and what history clearly reveals is that human culture has been intricately entwined with alcohol and other mood-altering substances. This trajectory follows three parallel and sometimes overlapping pathways: use for necessity and pleasure; use as a medicinal substance; and use as part of a religious ritual. Some substances, such as alcohol, fit in all three of these categories while others, such as peyote, are primarily used within a religious or spiritual context. Others, such as tobacco, were introduced as medicinal substances but quickly moved into the first category involving pleasure and conviviality.

## Necessity and Pleasure

The earliest evidence that exists concerning the production of alcoholic beverages is found in the form of clay pots dated from around 8000 BC (Standage, 2005). The inference can be drawn that the brewing of beer emerged as humans began to live in permanent settlements, thus creating the environment for fermentation. Later, beer is referenced in documents found in both ancient Mesopotamian and Egyptian civilizations that reveal the significance of beer as vital both for its antibacterial properties, making water suitable for drinking, and for its ability to make people feel better. In fact, beer was so valuable that for a time it served as a type of currency. There is ample evidence, for instance, that the workers who built the pyramids in Egypt were paid in beer (Standage, 2005, p. 27). The prominent role that beer played in Egyptian culture is exemplified in an ancient Egyptian proverb from around 2200 BC, "The mouth of a perfectly contented man is filled with beer" (Standage, 2005, p. 14; Gately, 2008, p. 5).

In addition, beer served as a distinguishing characteristic of civilization. As Standage (2005) elaborates, "the Mesopotamians regarded the consumption of beer and bread as one of the things that distinguished them from savages and made them fully human" (p. 27). The Mesopotamian epic of Gilgamesh is an example of this idea. Gilgamesh, a Sumerian king, was a man of civilization. In the course of events, he met Enkidu, a wild man of the forest, and they joined together to slay a demon in the forest. Enkidu's first encounter with civilization included being introduced to alcohol. "Enkidu ate the food until he was sated; he drank the beer – seven jugs! and became expansive and sang with joy!" (as quoted in Gately, 2008, p. 5). Thus began Enikidu's development from a wild to a civilized man.

While beer played a central role in ancient Egyptian and Mesopotamian civilizations, wine was also being produced, though it was reserved for the wealthy elite. By the time of Ancient Greece, however, wine played a central role in all strata of society and was used for offerings to the gods, as a currency, in rituals and convivial gatherings, and to assuage thirst (Gately, 2008, p. 11). Like beer, wine was used to make water potable, but its central role was that of communal connection. In fact, as Gately (2008) points out, in some Greek states, the consumption of wine was considered a civic duty (p. 11). Wine was generally mixed with water in various degrees of concentration, and it was considered barbaric to drink wine that was not mixed with water. The Ancient Greeks exported wine as far as southern France, the Crimean Peninsula and the Danube (p. 67). The Romans, who wholeheartedly adopted many aspects of Greek culture, extended the exportation of wine, seeing it not only as a sign of civilization but also as a means for better conquering indigenous tribes who were less formidable when they were intoxicated (p. 67).

The use of fermentation is evidenced in cultures throughout the world. In Mexico, tribes would travel great distances to find cacti whose fruit could be made into alcohol (Gately, 2008, p. 2). In China, evidence has been found dating back to 7000–6600 BC for a fermented drink that was made with rice, honey, grapes, and hawthorn berries (p. 2). And in the area now known as Iran, jars have been discovered that once held wine as well as other indications that mead, made from honey and beer, was also a mainstay.

Other substances also have served to provide social conviviality. Jay (2010) notes that kava, a substance that is imbibed in various forms to induce a sense of tranquility and ease of mind, is a central aspect of Polynesian culture. The use of kava is a means for maintaining culture values of generosity, sensitivity and conversation (p. 25).

## Medicinal

Part of the challenge in defining addiction is that many drugs are used instrumentally for a medicinal benefit. For example, the Ebers Papyrus, an ancient Egyptian medical text dating from around 1600 BC, describes the parts of the poppy plant and suggests it was recognized as an analgesic. Later texts from ancient Greece describe plants in terms of either cure or poison (Jay, 2010, p. 51). Likewise, tobacco, a New World import, took hold of European culture for its abilities to treat a variety of ailments. As Jay (2010) describes, "It could be chewed to treat stomach ailments, and the leaves applied topically for headaches" (p. 114).

The medicinal purposes of plants and their derivatives resulted in the development of a classification of substances for medicinal purposes in the 16th century by the Swiss alchemist and physician, Paracelsus. His intention was to transform Western medicine by basing the practice of medicine on chemical therapies. One such drug, "laudanum," which was probably a tincture of opium to help in pain relief, became so entrenched in common culture that it could be found on drug store shelves until it was removed in the 1930s by government edict (Jay, 2010, pp. 63–67).

During the mid-18th century, the classification of drugs was refined by Linnaeus, who had developed a renowned classification system of botany. Linnaeus's work on inebriants is the first modern classification of mind-altering drugs which included alcohol, poppy, and nightshade (Jay, 2010, p. 68). It is interesting to note that during his travels around Europe, Linnaeus was appalled at the excessive use of alcohol, particularly distilled liquor, he witnessed in the remote villages. He believed alcohol was by far the most destructive of the drugs in his classification. (p. 69).

At the beginning of the 19th century, a young German pharmacist's apprentice, Friedrich Sertürner, began to experiment with tarry opium, derived from the opium poppy, until he eventually isolated a compound that formed clear crystals. He named the compound morphine, after the god Morpheus, the Roman god of sleep (Jay, 2010, p. 77). This was the first plant to have given up a pure chemical substance. Like all drugs, morphine was a double-edged sword – it made modern surgery possible, but it also carried with it the potential for severe addiction. This breakthrough eventually resulted in the isolation of caffeine, nicotine, and codeine, which is found in the juice of the poppy head; and in 1860 the coca leaf would yield the stimulant cocaine (p. 78).

This standardization was the first step toward the emergence of modern drugs. From standardization emerged commoditization, the first of which was Dover's powder, created by Thomas Dover in 1732, a standardization of laudanum that was packaged to be easily displayed on the shelves of local grocers. Its removal in the 1930s signaled the beginnings of a more concerted effort on the part of the United States government to regulate powerful substances and make them less accessible to the general public.

Many of these drugs were used by individuals who wanted to experiment on themselves to better determine their effects. One such person was Sigmund Freud who hoped that cocaine would be an antidote to depression. During the 19th century, drugs were not yet stigmatized, and cocaine was sold as a remedy for almost any condition. The coca plant was used in the recipe for Coca-Cola which was advertised as a nerve tonic, and a cure for "hysteria, headaches and melancholia" (Jay, 2010, p. 92).

Eventually problems began to become apparent, though the line between medicinal and recreational use was still difficult to draw. However, by the beginning of the 20th century drug addiction was becoming a greater cause for concern. Jay (2010) notes that "In New York, addicts who sold scrap to feed their habits were known as 'junkies'" (p. 95). And eventually cocaine and morphine became illicit drugs sold by street-corner hustlers. He writes, "The public image of the drug user was changing from medical patient to dangerous thrill-seeker" (p. 95).

In 1914 the Harrison Narcotics Tax Act solidified the efforts to remove opiates and cocaine from the store shelves and limited them to medical use. This, in turn, stimulated efforts to create substitutes. In 1898, Bayer created a morphine substitute under the brand name of Heroin. This was soon withdrawn and eventually they launched Aspirin which took the share of headache pill market that opiates used to occupy.

In the 1880s chemists were investigating the alkaloids of ephedra and by 1927 the British pharmacologist, Gordon Alles, had synthesized a derivative he named amphetamine (Jay, 2010, p. 100). Amphetamines found their first major application during WWI when they were used to boost the endurance of soldiers and pilots in combat (p. 100). They were a popular over-the-counter pharmaceutical, but it did not take long for amphetamines to become recognized as a source of addiction and they, too, were placed in the category of controlled substances.

Almost all drugs that fall under the medicinal category have eventually revealed themselves to be highly addictive. Morphine made modern surgery possible, and its derivatives have been used to alleviate severe pain and thus diminish tremendous suffering. Amphetamines have been used most recently to treat attention deficit disorders. Similarly, cocaine did indeed lift the mood of a depressed individual but soon revealed itself to be so addictive that the cure was worse than the disease. But, unlike cocaine, which is primarily used as a topical anesthetic for eye surgery, morphine and other narcotics are a necessary part of modern medicine. Moreover, most people who use these medications do not become addicted to them.

## Use in Religious Ceremonies

In addition to conviviality, pleasure, and medicinal purposes, humans have also used psychoactive substances as part of religious ritual. Jay (2010) reports that among the earliest artifacts of hallucinogenic drug use are two chillum-style pipes excavated from the Andes and dating to before 2000 BC. These were found to contain residue of seeds that contain dimethyltryptamine (DMT) – a powerful, naturally occurring hallucinogen (p. 14). DMT is used to this day in shamanic rituals among the Amazonian indigenous cultures to induce immersion into a spiritual world. As Jay (2010) explains, the Amazon cultures that continue to use DMT typically describe the experience as terrifying (p. 16). Under the influence of hallucinogenic snuff, the shamans experience a state of hyper-consciousness and report being able to see, hear, smell, and understand aspects of reality that are normally not apparent (p. 20). This frequently consists of the use of hallucinogenic substances, such as peyote or DMT, with the intention of enabling allowing the individual to experience some form of transcendence or merging with the divine. In this case, most often the individual is accompanied by a guide who can interpret these experiences and also act as a stabilizing influence and a form of protection.

In the Western world, specifically in Ancient Greece, the rituals associated with the god Dionysus involved the use of wine for intoxication. No one knows what these rituals, called the Eleusinian mysteries, involved, as the details were a closely guarded secret, but it is said that those who went through the initiation lost their fear of death. The cult of Dionysus celebrated death and resurrection and offered a way for celebrants to counterbalance the cultural emphasis on the rational and logical. Similarly, in Ancient Egypt, Hathor, the goddess of fertility, was celebrated each year to coincide with the flooding of the Nile River during which time celebrants were encouraged to become intoxicated (Gately, 2008, p. 7).

Later on, Christianity would adopt the use of wine during its central ritual of the mass. From its inception, wine has been intimately associated with Christianity. Jesus's first miracle was turning water into wine at a wedding feast. In addition, wine was used at the Last Supper by Jesus as a symbol for the blood he would spill for the redemption of humanity. Thus the central ritual of Christianity, called the Eucharist, was established as a remembrance of this act and a sign of affiliation with the Church (Gately, 2008). But, unlike other rituals involving intoxicants, adherents were not seeking an ecstatic or mind-altering experience, but rather partaking, symbolically, in the suffering of Christ.

## Shifting Views on Intoxication

Even though mood- and mind-altering substances have been used instrumentally in various forms since the beginning of human civilization, the line separating use and abuse has also been a topic of debate and controversy. During the time of the Ancient Greeks, men who were habitual drunks, called *apeles*, meaning careless and/or carefree, were not disgraced, and in fact were honored with that title (Gately, 2008, p. 15). Those who drank too much were considered weak, though conversely, those who abstained from drinking alcohol were looked upon with suspicion (p. 15). The Greeks believed such people to be coldhearted and dangerous, lacking passion. Still, the Greeks recognized that drinking too much came with a high degree of risk, including death.

The Romans, venerating all things Greek, adopted a similar attitude toward drunkenness. Gately (2008) explains that the vast majority of Ancient Romans, and those they later conquered, saw relatively few reasons for not drinking regularly and in fact looked upon abstinence with suspicions. Some Germanic tribes, for example, refused to negotiate treaties unless all parties involved had gotten drunk together.

The first comprehensive attempt to institute moderation in drinking can be found in the writings of St. Paul who exhorted followers to avoid drinking alcohol "unworthily" (Gately, 2008, p. 43). Later, St. Clement of Alexandria (AD 150–215) wrote a detailed account concerning the consumption of wine wherein he argues that it was a sacred duty to drink wine as a sign of one's participation in the mystery of Christ's redemptive act. He emphasized that wine should be kept away from the youth, given its propensity to loosen inhibitions, and that adults should avoid drinking wine during meals and while at work. However, the elderly were advised to view it as an everyday drink as "the milk of old age" (p. 45). Clement painted a picture of those who disregarded his guidelines and became intoxicated as ugly, staggering, and vomiting (p. 45). In addition, he determined that women should not be allowed to drink wine, except as part of the Eucharist. This was in keeping with a long-standing proscription dating back to the time of Ancient Greece, that women were to be kept from drinking alcohol. During the Roman era there were very severe repercussions for those who did, including death. As Gately (2008) explains, "The wife of Egnatius Maetennus was clubbed to death by her husband for drinking from a large jar and he … was acquitted of murder by Romulus" (p. 29). This same historian reported, with approval, that a woman had been starved to death by her family for having "broken open the box containing the keys to the wine store" (p. 29). As we shall see, this particular antipathy toward women who drink alcohol continued well into the modern era, and it could be argued exists in some forms to this day.

Beer and wine continued to be mainstays of human civilization throughout the Middle Ages, during which time distillation of wine became more common. Brandy and later on rum became connected with the colonization of the Americas. In fact, rum was such an important part of daily life in the Colonial United States that its taxation was one of the precursors to the Revolutionary War.

A notable shift in human productivity can be observed with the introduction of coffee and tea as the preferred beverage first thing in the morning and throughout the day. As Standage (2005) relates, it became apparent that the average worker benefitted from drinking coffee; rather than arriving to work a bit logy from having drunk his morning beer, he now came to work energized and clearheaded (p. 139). This shift correlates with the emergence of the industrial revolution and subsequent technological innovations. Still, alcoholic beverages were mainstays of human culture then and now. While no longer needed to make water safe to drink, beer, wine, and distilled spirits were associated with conviviality, a connecting point in human enterprise and a source of pleasure.

## Learning to Enjoy the Substance

This points to a fact about the use of substances in general, which is that they are part of what Jay (2010) describes as the "web of verbal and symbolic culture" (p. 20). Thus, the meaning of the experience of taking the drug is just as important as the effect of the drug itself. The effects of the drug may initially be experienced as odd or unpleasant, until they are reframed as pleasurable and/or an expected part of the experience. This is the assertion put forth by Becker (1953) in a seminal paper on marijuana use. Becker observed that the initial use of marijuana was generally not experienced as pleasurable and thus "the novice has to be instructed as to the proper way to smoke the substance, but also to interpret the subsequence experience as pleasurable (p. 237). He quotes one of the participants in his study:

> I come back, "Hey, man, what's happening?" Like, you know, like I'd ask, "What's happening?" and all of a sudden I feel weird, you know. "Man, you're on, you know. You're on pot [high on marihuana]." I said, "No, am I?" Like I don't know what's happening.
>
> (p. 238)

The final stage requires the user to learn to enjoy the effects. As Becker (1953) explains:

> One more step is necessary if the user who has now learned to get high is to continue use. He must learn to enjoy the effects he has just learned to experience. Marihuana-produced sensations are not automatically or necessarily pleasurable. The taste for such experience is a socially acquired one, not different in kind from acquired tastes for oysters or dry martinis. The user feels dizzy, thirsty; his scalp tingles; he misjudges time and distances; and so on. Are these things pleasurable? He isn't sure. If he is to continue marihuana use, he must decide that they are. Otherwise, getting high, while a real enough experience, will be an unpleasant one he would rather avoid.
>
> (p. 239)

As Jay (2010) notes, this is the case with other substances. Alcohol, for example, does not appear to be innately satisfying, unlike sugar, for instance. Many of the symptoms of hallucinogenic mushrooms are taken for signs of toxicity until the user is schooled in viewing them as a "trip".

Recently, Becker's research has been evaluated in light of more current cultural realities by Hallstone (2002). He notes that while Becker's work is important, and in fact is one of the few studies of marijuana usage in the existing literature, Becker's outcomes have not been verified with regard to his three-stage model. Hallstone (2002) replicated Becker's research and found that the notion that one must be taught how to smoke marijuana and inducted into the experience has changed. His research found that fewer people reported needing to be introduced to the techniques of smoking marijuana due in large part to its increasing prevalence in general culture. This means that people have already been introduced to the idea long before they actually smoke their first joint. In addition, respondents indicated that their definition of getting high was based on the fact that they had an unusual experience. Thus the idea of what getting high means may have shifted over the years as well. In addition, a larger percentage of individuals reported getting high the first time they smoked marijuana than in Becker's study. This, too, is accounted for by increased prevalence of the drug as well as greater potency.

Acclimation to the use of mind- and mood-altering substances has its own process in history as they have been introduced from one part of the world to another. This is exemplified by Jay (2010) in his depiction of the introduction of alcohol to Native Americans. Like smoking tobacco for the Europeans, drinking alcohol was an entirely new practice for Native Americans. As Jay (2010) explains, "If a group of friends were given a bottle of rum, they would nominate one to drink it all rather than share it," thus contributing to the stereotype of the drunken Indian (p. 129). The understanding that drinking alcohol was a convivial experience, with each individual drinking from his own drinking vessel, had yet to be introduced.

This mirrors the experience of Europeans, for instance, who needed to learn to smoke tobacco which was imported from the New World. Tobacco initially took hold in Europe for its abilities to address various illnesses in a variety of forms. Despite the concern of some, including King James I of England who characterized tobacco use as an unhygienic habit spread by the vain and foolish, the use of tobacco continued to expand, particularly among soldiers as it relieved the boredom and stress of military life. Soon smoking and drinking became associated with leisure and companionship, particularly once the pipe was introduced, allowing individuals to smoke tobacco without necessarily having to share (p. 119).

## Conclusion

What history teaches us is that human beings are innately attracted to mind- and mood-altering substances. So much so that we cannot find evidence of any human culture that has not incorporated one or more of these into daily life. These substances, unlike food, water, and air, are not necessary to sustain life but, apparently, they are important nonetheless. The problem arises with the addictive qualities that are inherent in most of these substances – alcohol, morphine, cocaine, amphetamines – not for everyone, but for a significant minority of individuals. Addiction and alcoholism are destructive and life-threatening realities that society has attempted to address for centuries. How we have attempted to treat addiction in the United States is the topic to which we will now turn.

## One Alcoholic's Story

*An Alcoholic Through and Through*

> There is this to be said in favor of drinking, that it takes the drunkard first out of society, then out of the world.
>
> Ralph Waldo Emerson

I didn't have a dramatic childhood or anything. I think a lot of people want to focus on this happening, finding a reason for why you drink, but certainly that wasn't my case. When I was 16, I took my first drink and it was one of those deals where it stopped the anxiety, it slowed my mind down and my body. It was kind of a magical elixir and it removed all that stuff instantly. I literally thought I'd found the solution to my problems. It was that powerful. Sixteen is fairly late considering when most kids start but nonetheless it took effect and I proceeded to drink my way through high school. I controlled it – to the best of my ability. I knew it wasn't something you could do all the time but nonetheless I did it quite often and that continued throughout my school years. During that time, cocaine was everywhere and the friends I ran around with all did it and the parties so when the cocaine thing happened I got involved in that. I was able to put that down after a few years; it had a grip on me pretty strongly, but I was able to put that down and then the opiates came into play. I had that addictive personality that was always trying to find the new thing.

But my story is that I'm an alcoholic through and through and it would've killed me. I'm not under any delusion that I could go do cocaine, but the problem really is alcohol. With the opiates it was really the dependency and the same thing with the alcohol and I eventually got dependent on that as well. My first year in college I did really well, and my parents promised to get me a car as an incentive. But I wasn't able to sustain it; I just got too deep into my addiction. I also had a panic disorder kick in along with depression and that increased my alcohol intake to try to escape. It slows the neurons down. It helped in the short term, but it just prolonged the anxiety in the long haul. I saw some professional psychotherapists and there was one person in particular who said my problem wasn't the chemicals, it was the underlying disorders, but really it was both. So, I had both those things going on and started increasing my alcohol intake.

My first treatment was a forced situation at Hazelden when I was around 24, so a pretty good distance from 16. I'd dropped out of college but left in good standing. My brain was just running on empty and I wasn't doing myself any favors. I had gotten a DUI [Driving Under the Influence]. Some legal stuff started popping up. All my legal issues started when I started drinking and ended when I quit. I had been working for my dad and I was addicted to the opiates. I had been on a methadone program twice and wish I'd never gotten on it because I was drinking on it. Methadone combined with alcohol just wasn't going to work. I'd written a payroll check to get the money to buy some opiates and my dad had found out. So, he got me to go to Hazelden. I was an IV [intravenous] drug user at that time, so I said ok, I'll go, but before I left I put a syringe in the inside of my running shoe, under the insole, and superglued it together. Once I was in treatment, I had to struggle to get that syringe out of my shoe but ultimately, I did get it open and that lasted me about three days. They had me on a seven-day detox, so I'm using while I'm in detox.

I was doing anything to get out of there; it's in the middle of nowhere. My case manager got Dad on the phone who basically told me "If you come back here before finishing treatment, you're going to get arrested." So, I stuck with it and stayed there for about 35 days. I made it to the airport and was going to try to do this thing but ended up using the day I got back home, back to the opiates and then back to the alcohol – mostly using dilaudid. Like all alcoholics, in my innermost core, I thought I could control this stuff and that's what we alcoholics think we can do. I was working during this time, for my dad, and he and my mom helped out with rent, but they never gave me money. They had divorced at that time.

Two years later I went into another rehab at Sierra Tucson. After I discharged I came back and stayed sober for six weeks, maybe two months before I relapsed. So, I went back to Sierra Tucson. At this point I'm around 30 years old and I was living with a girl and I got her pregnant. She actually came to the family program and after that my son was born.

A year and half later things had gotten a whole lot worse. I was living out of my car; friends had gotten tired of me; my family was turning their locks when I came around; my grandmother was just uncomfortable when I came around. One day in November, I had half of half a gallon of alcohol and I was at a crossroads. It sounds like divine intervention, but I decided to give treatment another shot and somehow found Pacific Hills. So, I took a flight out there and detoxed for seven days in a local hospital. I was coming off benzos, methadone, and then the alcohol. I remember looking out the window at the Pacific Ocean and it was so beautiful but I'm shaking; I couldn't hold a spoon. After I detoxed, I went over to Pacific Hills, but I got scared there because I wasn't used to that kind of freedom; they were taking us outside to meetings and I was afraid I'd slip out to CVS and buy a bottle of liquor, so I ended up calling my dad and I took a cab out to Betty Ford. They were more of a closed environment; not quite a locked-down unit but almost. I went there for the 28 days and then my dad came and got me and took me back to Pacific Hills. So, I had back-to-back treatments.

Dad was supportive; anytime I asked for help my parents were always there. I did the program and moved into sober living and that was the first time I had followed the suggestion that a professional had made, and I think that was the difference. I was just willing to do whatever it took and just surrender and that was a big change for me. For whatever reason. I lived in sober living for about a year. I was seven years from initial treatment before I got 90 days of sobriety and it just doesn't have to be that hard. I was pretty hopeless at the beginning of that last treatment episode.

But looking back it was a combination of the treatment program. I conceded to my innermost self that I'm an alcoholic and I think in the DNA of every alcoholic/addict is that part of you that says, “I’m going to be able to control this.” I just had to get to that point where I realized that I just couldn’t do it. I had reached that incomprehensible demoralization stage. I remember one time after I was in sober living and another guy and I went into a Ralph’s supermarket. They had these big open bins of candy. In the past I would have just grabbed a handful of candy and put it in my mouth and I realized I just didn’t want to do that anymore. That was kind of the first honest thought I’d had in a long time; it seems like such a little thing to not just take what you want. But I had these little epiphanies. And then I was working with a therapist who I could tell anything to and he just didn’t freak out. He wasn’t judgmental. He’d just tell me, “You’re out of integrity with the program,” and let me figure it out. I was seeing him a couple of times a week and we did some family sessions with my parents.

Physically I was in such poor health; I had really high blood pressure and just horrific things but the cook at the facility let me borrow his bike, so I was biking everywhere; going to meetings; got my first sponsor and trying to do the things they suggested. My dad was coming out about once a month and we were doing therapy sessions. My therapist asked where I was going to live once I got back and no one had thought about that. I couldn’t live with my mom because we had a pretty tumultuous relationship. So, the therapist asked my dad if I’d be living with him, which was awkward at first because my dad had remarried but that’s what I did. Once I moved back, I just kept doing the things I was doing; I continued to work out and exercise. Eventually I started looking at college and finished that up and then I earned a master’s degree in social work. I always thought it would be cool to be a chemical dependency counselor. My therapist was a marriage and family therapist but really the degree didn’t really matter. It was what he provided to me that was the key. AA was so important but if I’d just had a sponsor it wouldn’t have been enough. Having a therapist who could work with me and my family really made the difference for me and now I’ve been sober for over 20 years.

## Questions for Discussion

1. The use of mind- and mood-altering substances follows three trajectories in human history: necessity and pleasure; medicinal; and religious ritual. Are there any other categories you can identify? Which substances can be found in all three? Which are found in only one?
2. Societal views on intoxication have shifted since the time of Ancient Greece. What was the perspective on intoxication during that time? When did this begin to shift? Where would you place our current views on intoxication? Are these views objective or culturally based?
3. The text discusses that idea that one needs to learn to use and enjoy most substances. What are your perspectives on this notion? Do you agree? Do you think that changing cultural mores and societal attitudes might affect this process? How?
4. What do you think there is about human nature that accounts for the consistent presence of mind- and mood-altering substances? What role might this play in society? What other reasons occur to you?

# 2

# THE HISTORY OF TREATMENT OF SUBSTANCE USE DISORDERS IN THE UNITED STATES

> I have absolutely no pleasure in the stimulants in which I sometimes so madly indulge. It has not been in the pursuit of pleasure that I have periled life and reputation and reason. It has been the desperate attempt to escape from torturing memories, from a sense of insupportable loneliness and a dread of some strange impending doom.
>
> Edgar Allan Poe

Though the use of mood- and mind-altering substances is ancient, the treatment of addiction is relatively modern. This chapter will provide a brief overview of the history of the treatment of Substance Use Disorders (SUDs) in the United States as well as an examination of current treatment models.

As we observed in the previous chapter, humans have had a long and entwined history with alcohol, opiates, hallucinogenic and other mood- or mind-altering substances. Thus, rather than being aberrant, the use of psychoactive substances is part and parcel of what it means to be human and is intimately connected to culture and civilization. This insight provides a window into the difficulties inherent in the treatment of addiction.

Part of this challenge lies in the fact that most people can use these substances without crossing the line into addiction. Alcohol is a prime example, since most people can use alcohol without long-term deleterious effects. And yet we know that there is a difference between occasional alcohol use and alcoholism. The same can be said for the use of opiates. Most individuals who use opiates, usually due to medical necessity such as surgery, do not become addicted to those medications. Other drugs, such as cocaine and meth-amphetamine, fall into a somewhat different category in that their use is rarely involved with medicinal purposes, though one could argue that Ritalin, a type of amphetamine, would fall into that category. But whether a substance is used for social enjoyment, as is the case for alcohol, or for pain management, or some other medically related purpose, these substances have the capacity to become addictive.

This raises the question as to how SUD is distinguished from use and even occasional abuse. Is the college student who regularly gets drunk on the weekends an alcoholic? Is the person who drinks heavily every evening but holds down a job? What about a person who has a chronic medical condition and regularly takes an opiate for the pain? Or the person with an anxiety disorder who takes an anti-anxiety medication every day?

## Defining Addiction

While definitions of addiction vary, there are several characteristics that are common to all. The definition given by the American Society for Addiction Medicine is as follows:

> Addiction is a primary, chronic disease of brain reward, motivation, memory and related circuitry. Dysfunction in these circuits leads to characteristic biological, psychological, social and spiritual manifestations. This is reflected in an individual pathologically pursuing reward and/or relief by substance use and other behaviors.

> Addiction is characterized by inability to consistently abstain, impairment in behavioral control, craving, diminished recognition of significant problems with one's behaviors and interpersonal relationships, and a dysfunctional emotional response. Like other chronic diseases, addiction often involves cycles of relapse and remission. Without treatment or engagement in recovery activities, addiction is progressive and can result in disability or premature death.
>
> (www.asam.org/resources/definition-of-addiction)

The *DSM-IV* (*Diagnostic Statistical Manual*) published by the American Psychiatric Association (2000) is the manual for diagnosis of all mental disorders. It defines addiction as a maladaptive pattern of substance use leading to clinically significant impairment or distress, as manifested by three (or more) of the following, occurring any time in the same 12-month period:

1. Tolerance, as defined by either of the following:
   (a) A need for markedly increased amounts of the substance to achieve intoxication or the desired effect. or
   (b) Markedly diminished effect with continued use of the same amount of the substance.

2. Withdrawal, as manifested by either of the following:
   (a) The characteristic withdrawal syndrome for the substance, or
   (b) The same (or closely related) substance is taken to relieve or avoid withdrawal symptoms.

3. The substance is often taken in larger amounts or over a longer period than intended.
4. There is a persistent desire or there are unsuccessful efforts to cut down or control substance use.
5. A great deal of time is spent in activities necessary to obtain the substance (such as visiting multiple doctors or driving long distances), use the substance (for example, chain-smoking), or recover from its effects.
6. Important social, occupational, or recreational activities are given up or reduced because of substance use.

7. The substance use is continued despite knowledge of having a persistent physical or psychological problem that is likely to have been caused or exacerbated by the substance (for example, current cocaine use despite recognition of cocaine-induced depression or continued drinking despite recognition that an ulcer was made worse by alcohol consumption).

The *DSM-V* represents a significant revision with regard to diagnosis, but essentially maintains the above-noted criteria while dividing the diagnostic criteria into specific categories designated by the type of substance (i.e., alcohol, cannabis, opiate, etc.). The general description found in the *DSM-V* for SUDs reads as follows:

> Overall, the diagnosis of a substance use disorder is based on a pathological pattern of behaviors related to use of the substance. To assist with organization, Criterion A criteria can be considered to fit within overall groupings of impaired control, social impairment, risky use, and pharmacological criteria.
>
> (doi-org.tcsedsystem.idm.oclc.org/10.1176/appi.books.9780890425596.dsm16)

The groupings include:

1. Impaired control, which includes increased use of the substance for the desired effect; persistent attempts to cut back or discontinue; a great deal of time spent in acquiring the substance, using, and recovering from use; craving and, in more severe cases, ordering one's entire life around the acquisition, use, and recovery.
2. Social impairment, which includes failure to fulfill work and personal obligations; persistent and recurrent interpersonal problems related to the use of the substance; giving up important work and social activities in order to maintain the use, and withdrawal from family and other activities.
3. Risky use, which includes continued use of the substance despite deleterious impact on one's work, family life, and physiology.

4. Pharmacological effects, including both tolerance and withdrawal. Tolerance is the ability to ingest increasingly greater amounts of the substance to achieve the desired effect; withdrawal is characterized by physical symptoms that occur when use is discontinued which can be life threatening.

Thus the defining characteristics of addiction are as follows:

1. A primary, chronic disease
2. Characterized by inability to consistently abstain
3. Impairment in behavior control
4. Inability to recognize the problems created by the substance use
5. Inability to regulate emotional response
6. Cycles of relapse and remission
7. Tolerance and withdrawal
8. Progressive disease that ends in premature death

It is important to recognize that these criteria represent a comprehensive picture of addiction which may also vary in individual cases. For example, not every individual who regularly drinks large amounts of alcohol will go through withdrawal if this is discontinued but that does not mean the individual is not an alcoholic. One would have to evaluate the individual in light of all the criteria.

In addition to SUDs, the *DSM-V* recognizes gambling as a behavioral addiction. For our purposes, we will define addiction in the larger sense which might include a behavioral addiction, but the focus will be on the use of substances.

## An Overview of Substance Use Disorder Treatment

White (2014) presents a detailed and comprehensive examination of the history of SUD treatment in the United States. I will present a synopsis of his work, but his work is well worth reading for its in-depth presentation of a long history. White (2014) begins with a discussion of Dr. Benjamin Rush, an influential figure in the founding of the United States, member of the Continental Congress, signer of the Declaration of Independence, and Physician-General of the Continental Army (p. 3). Rush's father was an alcoholic whose drinking led to his parents' divorce; this led to Rush's own interest in the treatment of alcoholism, and he was the first physician to subscribe to the disease concept. Rush identified the process and criteria of alcoholism, and recognized that this was transmitted intergenerationally within families. He also held that alcoholism, or drunkenness as it was then called, was "suicide perpetuated gradually," and postulated that there was some unconscious desire for self-injury underlying the disease. He was the first American physician to hold that complete abstinence was the only hope for an alcoholic, and he believed that permanent sobriety could be achieved only through a combination of "religious, metaphysical, and medical" influences (p. 5). Thus, Rush was almost prescient in his understanding of alcoholism, and his observations continue to hold true to this day.

By the early 1800s the temperance movement had begun, though even then there were two schools of thought: those who believed that moderated use could be achieved and those who argued for total abstinence. This movement was characterized by voluntary association aimed at helping people stay sober through a community of like-minded, struggling individuals. In addition, treatment clinics also emerged to address the physiological dangers of alcohol withdrawal and provide a foundation for recovery and sobriety. The first medically directed treatment facility was founded in New York in 1864. By 1909 there were nine facilities in the country (White, 2014, p. 34).

These early efforts in addiction treatment laid the foundation for our current practices, and generally included the following:

1. Isolation from the stressors and temptations of normal life
2. Some sort of detox regimen
3. Religious/spiritual practice
4. Social support from other patients, including the formation of clubs to support post-treatment
5. Work and recreation
6. Music therapy

7. Self-reflection or self-inventory
8. Acts of service to newly arrived patients by existing patients as service to the community.

It is interesting to note the absence of individual counseling and, more importantly, the neglect of the family. This is indicative of the ambivalence that still remains within the addiction treatment community toward the role of the family. White (2014) quotes Dr. H. H. Kane, who wrote in 1881:

> Very often the relatives, not understanding the meaning of certain symptoms, distressed beyond measure by the pitiful pleadings of the sufferer, will interpose and at once put an end to treatment, thus unwittingly and with well-meaning doing the patient injury of the gravest kind. (p. 55)

There were those who particularly blamed the wives of men in treatment as "the worst enemies an alcoholic has" (White, 2014, p. 56). This antipathy reflects the prevailing attitudes toward women which was reflected in the societal reluctance to recognize and treat alcoholism in women. As White (2014) explains, women who were alcoholics or addicts were either ignored or castigated. As a result, women frequently sought help for more socially acceptable illnesses such as neurasthenia, hysteria or melancholia. Mostly women hid their addictions through the use of medicines, many of which were high in alcohol content or contained other substances, such as opiates (p. 56). This attitude would continue to be a factor up into the present era, evidenced even in the generally inclusive Alcoholics Anonymous.

While initially reluctant, the medical community eventually attempted to address the issue of alcoholism and addiction. During the early 1900s public demand for medical institutions to address these issues became more pronounced. This shifted some of the focus away from religious and lay organizations and onto hospitals and related institutions. Just as is the case today, hospitals provided acute care but struggled to keep patients in treatment long enough to achieve some measure of sobriety (White, 2014, p. 119). But medical interventions have proved to be largely ineffective. Attempts to use drug therapies, morphine and sedatives in particular, only compounded the problem.

Other therapies, ranging from water cures, such as steam baths, wet packs and inhalers, to specialized diets, exercise, and nature walks were employed and discarded (p. 126).

Psychological interventions also arose with the advent of psychoanalysis as a formal theory of psychology. Freudian theory held that alcoholism was a failed strategy of self-help and impeded emotional maturation. Alfred Adler, a student of Freud and founder of the Individual Psychology theory, held that alcoholism was a result of overwhelming feelings of inferiority and social discomfort, while Karl Menninger saw alcoholism as a type of slow suicide (p. 131). Though these characterizations of addiction may be argued to be accurate, psychoanalysis was not suitable for treatment as it was too costly for most and ineffective even for those who could afford it (p. 133).

Lay therapy emerged in the wake of these treatment failures and is exemplified in the founding of the Emmanuel Clinic in Boston, Massachusetts in 1906. Founded by Reverend Elwood Worcester, the clinic required that alcoholics enter the program with the following caveats. They must have a personal desire to stop drinking. They must be willing to accept total abstinence as a goal and they must attend the initial interview fully sober and commit to not drinking for one week (White, 2014, p. 135). As White (2014) points out, the Emmanuel Clinic laid the groundwork for the future of alcoholism treatment. It integrated the fields of psychology and spirituality and was the first outpatient clinic to have psychological counseling as its primary intervention.

Other approaches, such as the one created by Richard Peabody, a recovering alcoholic who went on to study psychology, employed the use of relaxation techniques, guided visualization, and self-hypnosis to assist in stress management (White, 2014, p. 136). Peabody's book, *The Common Sense of Drinking*, was the main reference source for treatment professionals for many years. In this work, Peabody outlined three causes for alcoholism: 1. a physiological predisposition due to inherited familial traits; 2. the effects of the early family environment, and 3. the influence of external stressors (p. 136). Peabody blamed parents, particularly mothers, as the primary causative factor, believing that maternal domination, combined with passive fathering, results in feelings of helplessness and inferiority (p. 137). Peabody trained lay counselors in his approach, which was employed as the standard treatment until well into the 1950s and, in fact, one could argue, remains so to this day.

In 1962, the United States Supreme Court declared that drug addiction was a disease, and to punish someone for being an addict was unconstitutional (White, 2014, p. 374). This underscored a broad acceptance of the disease model of addiction both in public policy and in popular culture. Legislation soon followed to address the issues of alcoholism and addiction culminating in 1970 with the Comprehensive Alcoholism Prevention and Treatment Act. This established the National Institute on Alcohol Abuse and Alcoholism (NIAAA) and as White (2014) states, "transformed this social movement into a new industry" (p. 378). A few years later the National Institute of Drug Abuse (NIDA) was established under the auspices of the National Institute of Mental Health (NIMH). The influx of large amounts of federal funds, combined with the acceptance of the disease model by the insurance industry, resulted in an exponential increase in drug treatment programs (p. 378).

By the 1980s the standard treatment program consisted of medical detoxification, group-oriented counseling, psychoeducation groups, physical fitness, and attendance at AA meetings with the standard of 28-day inpatient treatment followed by a short term aftercare program. Those who provided care were a combination of physicians, psychotherapists, and ex-addict counselors. This latter group were often newly sober with little to no training, resulting in a high rate of relapse among these workers. Eventually formal training for drug addiction counselors emerged with the founding of the National Association of Alcoholism Counselors and Trainers (NAACT), the National Association of Alcoholism Counselors (NAAC), and the National Association of Alcoholism and Drug Abuse Counselors (NAADAC). This was paralleled by the emergence of addiction medicine which resulted in the creation of the American Society on Alcoholism and Other Drug Dependencies (ASAM) (White, 2014, p. 391).

## Current Treatment Standards

By 2012, there were more than 16,000 treatment programs in the United States for alcoholism and drug addiction (White, 2014, p. 424). Federal and state agencies oversee these services with a combination of accreditation of the programs and licensure or certification of those who provide the treatment. In addition, the 21st century has seen a call for evidence-based treatments (EBTs) and systems to assure that programs are effective and that outcomes are measurable. Some interventions emerged from this research as effective, including brief counseling, cognitive behavior therapy, community reinforcement approach, behavioral marital therapy, contingency management, while others were discredited (educational lectures and films, boot camps, confrontation-based approaches) (p. 434). However, as White (2014) notes, "Recent reviews of the state of addiction treatment generally revealed the growth of evidence-based treatment options but the lack of full integration of EBTs into mainstream addiction treatment" (p. 434).

Treatment standards put forth by the NIDA state that 90 days of professional support across all levels of care is best to support recovery. This standard, however, is not routinely adhered to, with many treatment episodes averaging far less time. White (2014) notes that a meta-analysis of addiction treatment studies reveals approximately 50% of individuals completing addiction treatment resume using their drug of choice within one year (p. 435). And these are the individuals who completed treatment. Only 44% of those who start treatment complete the program (p. 434). In addition, though research supports connecting individuals in treatment with community resources, particularly 12-step groups, approximately 50% of clients report that they did not attend a single recovery support meeting following discharge (p. 434). This is particularly true for adolescents and young adults. This is problematic because, as White (2014) explains, "Long-term recovery outcomes are influenced more by extra-treatment than intra-treatment factors" (p. 435). In addition, research indicates that post-treatment monitoring and support can strengthen long-term outcomes, but only one in five adults receives this extended care. The challenge in providing such care lies in the fact that sustained recovery is not reached until four to five years post-treatment; while this may seem daunting, White (2014) points out that this parallels treatment rates for other chronic illnesses such as cancer (p. 435). Thus it appears that a shift in perspective is needed with regard to addiction. While the disease model has been generally embraced by the addiction treatment community and society as a whole, the misunderstanding of the nature of this disease may be reflected in the lack of post-treatment protocols.

One reason that accounts for the challenges in treating addiction lies in the difficulty addicts and alcoholics face in maintaining recovery. The average remission/recovery rate remains around 50% one year after treatment. Of these, most will relapse within 90 days of discharge (p. 435). This highlights the ongoing challenge of effectively addressing the complex issues that surround alcoholism and drug addiction.

A review of research and publications on substance abuse treatment quickly reveals the absence of consensus. As a result, research outcomes regarding the efficacy of treatment are compromised because no two treatment programs are alike. It is possible, however, to determine in broad strokes what the standard treatment programs tend to utilize. The website for the Substance Abuse and Mental Health Services Administration (SAMHSA (samhsa.gov/treatment/substance-use-disorders)) lists the following components of substance abuse treatment:

- Individual and group counseling
- Inpatient and residential treatment
- Intensive outpatient treatment
- Partial hospital programs
- Case or care management
- Medication
- Recovery support services
- 12-Step fellowship

Thus, treatment can include some or all of these components depending on the nature and severity of the addiction. White (2014) notes that NIDA issued a set of 13 principles of addiction treatment. Among these are the assumptions that no single treatment is appropriate for everyone, and that effective treatment attends to multiple needs of the individual, not just his or her drug abuse (p. 431).

In recent years, much attention has been given to the multiple factors involved in alcoholism and drug addiction with regard to not only efficacy of specific treatment interventions but also the philosophical foundations of treatment itself. These include questioning the assumption that an individual does not seek treatment because they are not in enough pain; evaluating the view that addiction is a chronic disease; investigating Harm

Reduction (HR) approaches such as distribution of methadone; and determining whether or not moderate drinking is even an appropriate goal of treatment (White, 2014). The debate over these and many other subjects continues to influence treatment and public policy.

## Conclusion

A review of the current treatment standards and research surrounding the efficacy of treatment clearly reveals that there is a lack of consensus. While treatment programs tend to look very similar to one another in that they employ the same types of interventions, the paucity of research outcomes makes it difficult, if not impossible, to determine which interventions are most likely to effectuate lasting recovery.

It has been argued that alcoholism and addiction should be viewed as a chronic illness, like diabetes or cancer. Recent innovations in treatment for these conditions have made it possible to create treatment protocols that are unique to the individual. As White (2014) maintains "I would further add that the highest quality of treatment involves not merely choosing the right program for the right client, but choosing the right program for the right client at the right time" (p. 520). Understanding the developmental aspect of readiness for change, and evaluating clients in that light, would fit with this assumption.

In addition to institutional treatment programs, White (2014) also proposes that the approach to treatment of addictions be similar to that of other mental disorders. This would offer a greater breadth of services to help sustain recovery after the completion of a formal treatment program. What this type of system would look like is the topic for a different book. But what the research demonstrates is that in the past 200 years of treatment for alcoholism and addiction, the insights and interventions of family systems therapy have never been utilized. The FMP represents an effort to address this by meeting the needs of the individual struggling with addiction and the family system. First, however, a review of the history of Alcoholics Anonymous and the 12-step movement is important in order to set the program within the larger context of treatment options.

## One Addict's Story

*AA through the Back Door*

> Habit is habit, and not to be flung out of the window by any man, but coaxed downstairs a step at a time.
>
> Mark Twain

I grew up with two parents who were addicts. My mom had me when she was 16 years old; she and my Dad moved in together and tried to make it work, but my Dad became abusive, so they separated. After that, my mom and I moved in with my grandparents. They provided a lot of stability for me. Being around alcoholics and the lack of boundaries meant that I endured emotional, physical, mental, and sexual trauma as a child. Eventually, my mom got remarried to a man she met in rehab and she and my stepfather came and took me to live with them. That was really disruptive, and confusing; it was a tough time for me.

The first time I got drunk I was a freshman in high school. My friends and I were at Downtown Disney and I got so drunk that I blacked out and was arrested for being drunk in public. When I was in my sophomore year, I was at a party and drank so much that I blacked out, again. I got picked up by the cops for being intoxicated and was taken to the drunk tank. About a year later, during my junior year, I was at a party and a bunch of us decided to leave. We all got into a car and as we were driving, I remembered I'd left a big bottle of alcohol at the party. I urged everyone to go back and, on the way, we got into a big accident. Everyone in the car was severely injured except me. One of my friends suffered a serious brain injury. My Mom came and started yelling at me; I was crying and feeling terrible. As a punishment, she wouldn't allow me to go and visit my friends in the hospital. I carried a lot of shame and guilt about the accident for years afterwards because I felt it was my fault for having convinced everyone to go back to the party. Despite the shame and guilt, I remember being interviewed about the accident for our local news station and the reporter asked if I would be drinking again and I said, "Yes! Of course!" That's how naïve I was!

During my teens, my Mom became successful and was able to provide a lot of things for me, but I was really struggling emotionally and was suicidal, though I never told anyone. Finally, I told my Mom that I wanted to see a therapist, but she never did anything about it. So, I finally contacted a therapist and started seeing her regularly. In fact, I still see her to this day. I eventually told her about my suicidal thoughts and disclosed to her that I had attempted suicide twice before. During this time by parents' marriage was chaotic and they were fighting a lot. I remember that I felt responsible for my little brother, who was born when I was 15 years old; I wanted to protect him, but I didn't know how. I was still drinking a lot and between that and my parents' fighting to the point where the cops were called a couple of times, it was just too overwhelming. On top of that my Mom had started using again and started engaging in some shady business practices, which we found out about later.

I wanted to go to college but instead I ran away and lived in a friend's garage with some other people. Her parents didn't seem to mind that we were drinking and smoking in there. I ended up getting a full-time job even with all this going on. My mom ended up in jail a few times for her drug use. She finally got pulled over for a DUI and was facing prison time, so she gave up her US citizenship and moved to Mexico. This whole thing was so painful for me because I loved my Mom, and I felt a sense of responsibility for her. She seemed to do OK for a while when she first moved to Mexico, but then she found a boyfriend who enabled her drug use. I stayed in contact with her during this time, but it was hard. Two years ago, I was notified that she was in a coma in ICU and she ended up passing away after being in a coma for a week.

When my mom was still alive, I was able to stay in contact with her, but I had my boundaries; I didn't give her money, even though I was scared she'd be mad at me. I just knew I couldn't jump on the crazy train anymore. I learned to detach with love which is something I learned in Al-Anon. I got into AA through the back door. I first attended Al-Anon at the recommendation of my therapist. While I was going to Al-Anon, they recommended that I attend an AA meeting to find out what it's like to be an alcoholic and while I was at the AA meeting and listened to the stories, I realized that I couldn't stop using alcohol either. So, I started attending AA and got a sponsor. I relapsed a lot in the first year and a half but every time I drank, I'd end up really depressed the next day. I called in sick to work a lot and I was scared of losing my job. One day I went out with a friend to celebrate her birthday and I had resolved not to drink. Instead I ended up in a blackout, waking up at some guy's house, not knowing how I even got there. Two of my friends were also there and they said I'd acted fine the night before. That incident is something I refer to when my alcoholic mind tells me I don't have a problem. I could not stop drinking based on my own good thinking and good intentions.

My eating disorder came out when I attempted to get sober from alcohol, and I thought that sobriety was the reason I could not control my eating any longer, so I left AA and tried to do it on my own. I got into bodybuilding and my boyfriend at the time got into it with me as well. By this time, I had started drinking again, blacking out, becoming resentful and jealous. One day, we went to a wedding and I became really paranoid that other women were hitting on him. I became depressed and suicidal, and that was my emotional bottom. I knew I couldn't and didn't know how to do life or have a healthy relationship. He suggested I go back to AA meetings because I had been so much happier then. I resisted at first but finally I went and did it all – 90 meetings in 90 days – I was desperate. I had some struggles along the way; I had to address my eating disorder a couple of years into my sobriety, and I found out I also needed to be part of Sex and Love Addicts Anonymous, and it ended up that my sex and love addiction was the hardest thing for me to give up because it was the only way I felt validation. I continued to work the program and to see my therapist, which helped me stay sober during these tough times. The years of therapy have helped me uncover, discover, and discard things about my past that kept me reliving self-defeating patterns that I could not stop. Recently, after my Mom passed away, I was given the ability to grieve. I was able to cry and be with my feelings regardless of how painful it was, which I was not able to do before without acting out in inappropriate ways. Today I am six months pregnant and looking forward to being a mother and stopping the negative chain of addiction and trauma that has been passed down. I'm going to school to become a psychologist and am working part-time as a certified nutritionist at treatment facilities. I am using the wounds I have endured throughout my life to give me direction in my life, and I couldn't be more grateful for it all.

### Questions for Discussion

1. This chapter reviews the criteria for addiction. How would you distinguish between an alcoholic and a social drinker? What would let you know if someone has crossed the line into alcoholism?
2. The disease model of addiction has been adopted by the medical community, treatment facilities, and the US Government Department of Health and Human Services. Still, there is some controversy concerning this assumption. Some individuals argue that addiction is a learned behavior. Others that it is a compulsion. What are your views on this? What difference do you think it makes regarding treatment?
3. The efforts to create a formal approach to treatment began in the mid-1800s in the United States. When you review the treatment format that was implemented in those early days, what comes to mind? What similarities do you see to current practices? Are there any differences?
4. The text notes that women were treated differently regarding addiction and alcoholism. How do you account for this? Does this continue to exist? If so, in what ways?

# 3

# ALCOHOLICS ANONYMOUS

> Going from being the person that people were repulsed by, being randomly searched all the time, to what I have now it's all from the program and from sobriety. These are the tangible benefits. Those intangible things – the love and the trust – that's the proof that what I'm doing is working. And it's getting better all the time. I'm 13½ years clean and sober; I have a great job and a future; I'm married. I have a rich, full life.
>
> One Addict's Story

It is impossible to speak about the efforts to address alcoholism and drug addiction without understanding the impact of Alcoholics Anonymous. Though this topic fits into the historical overview presented in the previous chapter, the influence of AA and the 12-step movement is so significant that it requires a chapter of its own. As White (2014) states, "No recovery mutual-aid movement before or after AA has reached more alcoholics, been more widely adapted to address other problems, sustained itself so long, nor more profoundly influenced the evolution of addiction treatment" (p. 169). It is a testament to AA that almost every addictions treatment program includes participation in a 12-step program.

## Beginnings

While the lineaments of AA can be seen in the mutual aid societies of the past, the creation of the formal program can be traced to the mid-1920s. While there are many streams of influence involved in the creation of AA, a definitive nodal event occurred in 1926 when a well-to-do American businessman, Rowland Hazard, sought help for his alcoholism from Carl Jung, the Swiss psychoanalyst and founder of Analytic Psychology. Despite his year-long analysis with Jung, Hazard soon relapsed. Seeking to return to his work in analysis, Hazard was informed by Jung that, in his opinion, neither medical nor psychiatric treatment would work. Instead, Jung stated that he believed Hazard's only hope was to have a transformative spiritual experience. According to Jung, alcoholism is a response to a spiritual vacuum, and psychotherapy could not provide the environment for such an experience. In response to this, Hazard began searching for a group that might open the door to a spiritual awakening. He found this in the Oxford Group, a spiritual movement that had begun in the 1920s and held that the problems of this world could only be healed through personal spiritual change.

According to White (2014) the Oxford Group held to four ideals – absolute honesty; absolute purity; absolute unselfishness; and absolute love. In addition, they held to five processes – give in to God; listen to God's direction; check guidance, restitution, and sharing through witness (p. 170). The group's emphasis on spiritual surrender, which included admitting that one was powerless over alcohol, relying on God as a source of strength, confessing one's wrongs, creating a moral self-inventory and helping others, greatly impacted Hazard. He, in turn, passed these insights along to his friend Ebby T., who was also in the throes of alcoholism and who, as a result of his experience with the Oxford Group, also found release. Ebby eventually passed this along to Bill Wilson, who was in the midst of a severe addiction to alcohol and on the verge of being committed to a psychiatric institution.

While in treatment at a hospital for detox, Bill W. experienced a deeply meaningful experience of transcendence in which, after crying out to God to reveal himself, he describes seeing a bright light that enveloped him and brought with it a feeling of freedom and ecstasy. Seeking to assure himself that he was not hallucinating, Bill W. checked with his physician, Dr. William Silkworth, who assured him that he had indeed experienced a spiritual breakthrough. This confirmation proved to be life-changing. Later, Bill W. met Dr. Robert Smith, or Dr. Bob, and the two began the slow, tentative creation of a new movement that came to be known as Alcoholics Anonymous. Though informed by some of the tenets of the Oxford Group, AA with its emphasis on alcoholics soon moved in a different direction.

AA incorporates many of the ideas that others had implemented in various ways: the disease model of alcoholism; the admission that an alcoholic is powerless over alcohol and the only way to achieve lasting sobriety is through a spiritual awakening; sharing of personal experiences; those with more experience assisting those who are just starting out. In addition, as White (2014) points out, there are many behavioral and cognitive prescriptions that are part of the AA program – don't drink, go to meetings; get a sponsor; work the steps; practice meditation; use thought stopping; find substitutions; and become active in a larger community (p. 193).

The early days of AA featured some experimentation before the 12 steps and Twelve Traditions were established and the organization settled into its current form. At one point, Bill W. imagined that AA might move into more formal treatment with the founding of AA hospitals but this idea was generally discouraged as detracting from the volunteer principles of AA. Still, the issue about how best to go about detox was a source of debate in the AA community throughout the 1940s. And while there was no formal effort to create a detox program, AA did provide a major influence on how hospitals implemented detox programs. This also dovetailed with the movement, within the medical community and the culture as a whole, away from the moral failure model of alcoholism and toward embracing the disease model as it stands today (White, 2014, p. 220).

The emphasis on pure volunteerism and mutual support was firmly established by an unlikely source, the wealthy philanthropist John D. Rockefeller, Jr. Though he had been approached with a request for a grant of $50,000, Rockefeller instead placed $5,000 in the treasury of the Riverside Church to help pay the AA founders' living expenses during the early days of the organization. Rockefeller's concern that too much money would spoil the spontaneity of the movement proved to be prescient and current AA literature acknowledges "Rockefeller's refusal saved AA from itself" (White, 2014, p. 175). Instead, AA created an Alcoholic Foundation in 1938, consisting of two alcoholic members and three non-alcoholic members to provide oversight for the movement.

The publication in 1939 of *Alcoholics Anonymous* or the "Big Book" furthered the growth of the AA movement and is still the primary text of AA. Its nickname came from the fact that the original publication was printed on heavy paper stock to allow alcoholics who might struggle with tremors to turn the pages, making the book unusually large. Concurrent with this was the more gradual development of rules and rituals for meetings (White, 2014, p. 177).

Some practices arose organically. For example, the idea of sponsorship arose from the early practice of one member guaranteeing payment of the hospital bills of a new member. This was formalized in its current iteration in the 1940s, though even now there are some differences of opinions with regard to the role of a sponsor. Some have argued for sponsorship as short-term role, mainly for introducing new members to the group. Others have conceptualized sponsorship as more permanent, though there was always leeway to switch sponsors along the way.

In the early days of AA, differences in ideas and perspectives resulted in groups splitting off from one another. Accusations were made that Dr. Bob and Bill W. were becoming wealthy from the proceeds of the Big Book, conflicts arose over the use of money, the misuse of the AA name, etc. As a result, Bill W. began to conceive of a set of codes to govern the organization. These evolved into what is now known as the Twelve Traditions. During this time, the organization's newsletter the *AA Grapevine* began publication, initially aimed at members of the armed services, but gradually expanding to all AA members. As White (2014) explains, this, along with the Twelve Traditions, helped guide AA during a period of rapid growth (p. 179). These were formalized with the publication of the book *Twelve Steps and Twelve Traditions* in 1953 by the AA publishing company, AA Worlds Services, Inc. (p. 182).

While change was the byword for the AA movement during this time of growth, what did not change was Bill W.'s quest to find ways to help people who were struggling with alcoholism, particularly those who had not been able to achieve sobriety through the AA program. At one point, he explored the possibility that LSD might assist individuals in experiencing the spiritual transformation that is at the heart of recovery through the AA model. He himself experimented and reported that his first experience had produced a spiritual experience. As White (2014) explains, "As late as 1967, the *AA Grapevine* reported on studies that showed positive results from using LSD in the treatment of alcoholism" (p. 185).

Underlying all of Bill W.'s efforts was his continued commitment to the AA model, centering on his awareness of the need to maintain humility, and his willingness to correct his path when it strayed into areas that might compromise this commitment. As a result, AA was able to grow beyond the personality of Bill W. and continue to operate long after he had turned the day-to-day governance of the organization over to the General Service Board (White, 2014, p. 185). Bill W. died in 1971 of emphysema, leaving behind a legacy of hope and help for others struggling with alcoholism and addiction.

## The Program of Alcoholics Anonymous

In order to fully understand AA and what it means to work the steps, experience always trumps intellectual understanding. Attendance at AA meetings available to all in "open" meetings, or one of the many corollary 12-step groups such as Al-Anon (for family members of alcoholics), CoDA (co-dependents anonymous), or Nar-Anon (for family members of addicts) is highly recommended. As White (2014) rightly notes, despite its prevalence, AA remains controversial and it is not unusual for individuals who have had limited to no experience of AA to put forth strong negative opinions about the value of AA (p. 190).

While AA does maintain that an individual must have some sort of spiritual transformation in order to maintain sobriety, it is not a religious organization. It does not hold to any specific view of theology, using the terms "higher power" and "God as we understand him." This is in keeping with the idea proposed by Carl Jung and others that alcoholism is a disease with spiritual implications and thus only a spiritual awakening can counter the power of the disease.

So what is the AA program? As White (2014) points out, it is essentially contained within the 12 steps. Practices may vary somewhat from group to group, but what defines AA fundamentally is the adherence to each member's commitment to "working" the steps. White (2014) explains that AA distinguishes between not drinking and sobriety. Not drinking is abstinence from a harmful substance; sobriety involves a spiritual transformation and a change of personal identity so that alcohol is no longer the center of existence. This involves four elements: 1. Surrender; 2. Identification; 3. Hope; and 4. Daily prescriptions for living (White, 2014, p. 192).

AA holds that alcoholism is a disease over which the individual has no control; it also holds that the disease is progressive and fatal. Though you can never be cured of the disease, i.e., become someone who can drink normally, you can reconstruct your identity and lifestyle so that drinking is no longer the focus of your life. You do this by a daily program of surrender to a higher power and by maintaining your spiritual journey. Thus surrender is the key to sobriety. As White (2014) notes, the paradox inherent in this is that by admitting to absolute failure (to control his or her drinking) the alcoholic succeeds.

Surrender, in turn, opens an individual to identification with the AA community and provides the basis for hope in transformation. Thus, the language of AA is "we" rather than "I." The prescriptions for achieving sobriety are clearly laid out and are both cognitive and behavioral (White, 2014, p. 193). Don't drink; got to meetings; get a sponsor; read the Big Book; work the steps. The focus is on one 24-hour period – the slogan "One day at a time" encapsulates this. The wisdom of this lies in the understanding that "never" is an overwhelming amount of time, but one hour or one day seems achievable. Thus the commitment is for a day, "You can do anything today but drink: Do Anything! But don't take the first drink!" (White, 2014, p. 193).

The ritual of introduction at AA meetings, i.e., "My name is ________. I'm an alcoholic," signals the change in personal identity. One is now identifying oneself as an alcoholic, which is in itself a significant change. But the process of identifying reconstruction is a gradual one achieved through attending to each of the steps and putting them into whatever action may be required. Over time, someone who is active in the process of sobriety inherent within the 12 steps will change in some important and fundamental ways.

This also positively affects all areas of an AA member's life. Personal relationships can be restored through the process of creating a searching moral inventory, asking for forgiveness, and making amends. This assists the member in releasing guilt and shame through actively restoring harmony and then letting go of the guilt. In addition to positively affecting personal relationships, AA also assists members in reconstructing their lifestyle. For most, this is a shift away from a lifestyle that was organized around and focused on the alcohol and replacing this with various components of the AA program. AA does this in a variety of ways, including rituals involving the telling of one's story, i.e., who the individual was before joining AA and who they are now; the role of slogans, i.e., "one day at a time"; "let go and let God"; "first things first"; and the role of laughter that comes from seeing oneself in the stories of others and identifying with them (White, 2014, pp. 195–196).

Finally, the idea of giving back to others is a central component of the 12 steps of AA. Often this takes the form of sponsorship, but it is not limited to this role. Implicit within this final step of the 12 steps is the recognition that the individual has something to contribute to the well-being of others and that doing so can help balance the scales. This is reminiscent of the Navajo idea of "hozho" which encompasses the idea of walking in peace, harmony, and beauty. When an individual does something that injures another member of the community, he or she is out of harmony and can suffer as a result. Doing something to balance the scales can restore harmony to the individual and the community. A similar idea can be found in the Catholic rite of reconciliation or confession. This is done to bring the individual back into right relationship with him- or herself and others. The healing power of such a ritual is attested to by the fact that it exists in many forms across cultures and has remained to this day. Thus, the culmination of the AA 12 steps assists the individual in restoration to one's self, one's relationships and one's community.

There are other aspects of the AA program that are important to note. The emphasis on anonymity was started early in the organization's history and allowed for a sense of safety, helping to counter the stigma of alcoholism. In addition, AA has eliminated the economic and social barriers by insisting that all meetings be free of charge and that there be no membership criteria. AA has maintained its emphasis on alcoholics, though others may attend who are struggling with other forms of addiction. But probably the most significant aspect of the AA philosophy is the idea of focusing on a spiritual awakening, one which is open to personal interpretation. Without this fundamental assumption, the other steps do not make sense, as it could be argued that they are predicated on the notion of giving up the illusion that the individual is the "god" of his or her own universe and surrendering to something that is experienced as transcendent.

## Criticisms of Alcoholics Anonymous

Any organization as large and influential as AA will have its detractors. Sometimes the criticisms lodged against AA have some legitimacy but most of the common criticisms come from those who are not fully informed about the program. Though White (2014) offers a more comprehensive exploration of this topic, I will include a few of the most common criticisms in this section (pp. 204–206).

Probably the most frequently cited criticism of AA, particularly among mental health professionals, is the lack of empirical research on the efficacy of the program. The fact is that there have been a number of studies on this topic and while the anonymity of AA can limit the way in which data is collected, research is still able to be conducted under those circumstances. In addition, it is important to keep in mind that research on addiction treatment in general is limited and incomplete.

Another criticism of AA involves its insistence on a spiritual awakening and reliance on a higher power. Some have argued that this has presented a barrier to those who are atheists. As White (2014) explains, however, studies have shown that individuals with an absence or low degree of religiosity are just as likely to be active in AA as those with a high degree of religiosity (p. 204). In general practice, one's higher power is self-defined, not defined by the organization. In addition, what constitutes a spiritual awakening is also open to personal interpretation. Alcoholics and addicts have already experienced giving themselves over to a higher power – their drug of choice. This "higher power" has been the focus of their existence; has demanded everything from the individual – time, money, relationships, and ultimately their life. Changing from the drug or alcohol as the higher power to one that seeks the best interest of the individual as defined by AA is really the focus of membership in AA and other 12-step organizations.

A third criticism is that AA members have just switched dependency from alcohol to AA. A corollary complaint is that AA is a cult that brainwashes its members. While AA does fill the void that is left by the removal of alcohol and other drugs, it can be argued that regular attendance at AA meetings is not much different than regularly attending religious services at a house of worship or regularly attending meetings of a service organization or public advocacy group. This criticism is one that is frequently leveled by a family member, often a spouse, and can be understood as a change-back reaction of the family system that is more comfortable with the individual in his or her addiction than in sobriety.

The disease model that is held by AA is also regularly criticized as a means for avoiding responsibility. AA members are exhorted to take responsibility for their behaviors and to put such responsibility into action. While someone who is not a member of a 12-step organization may use the disease model as an excuse to avoid sobriety, this is not the view of AA or other 12-step organizations.

Another possibly more significant criticism of AA is that it is primarily an organization for affluent white males. White (2014) offers an extensive overview of the history of AA regarding this issue but I will briefly summarize the context for this in the following section.

The history of women with regard to alcoholism and addiction has been a troubled one, as there has been a cultural denial mixed with hostility that is in some ways more intense than that directed toward men. While this has lessened to a large degree, it can be argued that aspects of this continue to linger into the modern era. This historical and cultural antipathy toward female alcoholics can be seen in the earliest days of the AA movement but there are also other reasons for the debate over the role of women in AA, both as support figures and as those who struggle with alcoholism.

As White (2014) notes, despite the significant contribution of Anne Smith and Lois Wilson, the wives of founders Dr. Bob and Bill W., many early AA members did not believe women could be alcoholics, or were simply uncomfortable around female alcoholics. The controversy included some of the wives of members who felt threatened by the inclusion of females in the group and this was a concern that was shared by others. The infamous "thirteenth step" is a reflection of this concern, and unfortunately based on factual experience, in which a member has a sexual or romantic relationship with another newly sober member which destabilizes the new-found sobriety.

The fear of potential sexual dynamics is a legitimate one and in the early years, women and men sat on different sides of meeting room. Difficulties emerged when female alcoholics were in search of a sponsor and at first this was provided by one of the wives of the alcoholics if no other female was available. Over time, however, this practice was discontinued. The creation of single gender groups in addition to mixed groups allowed for more choice in selecting a group that best fits with the individual's needs.

As White (2014) explains, the general attitudes toward women were somewhat mirrored in AA, though mitigated by the factors inherent in the AA organization which eventually led to a resolution. Assumptions concerning women included indictments such as: women form attachments that are too intense; women want to run things; women talk too much; few women can think abstractly; women who attend groups are on the prowl for men; too many women can't get along with the wives of members (p. 208).

As a result, women had to fight their way through these assumptions and persevere in order to participate. As White (2014) points out, some of the intensity of these concerns can be attributed to the ongoing fear that something would come along and destroy AA (p. 208). Women did eventually overcome these stigmas, and contributed a great deal to the development of the organization.

In addition to women, people of color also faced challenges that mirrored those they faced in the larger culture. In some areas, African Americans created their own groups because they were denied formal membership by existing, all-white groups. Because of the issues of segregation, AA as an organization deferred to local groups. Eventually, AA became fully integrated, with greater availability to the African American community.

Latinos were included early on and in 1940 the Big Book was translated into Spanish. Current AA literature includes pamphlets regarding women, native Americans, and gay/lesbian individuals. A significant percentage of AA is female, between 33% and 35% in the United States, though surveys conducted by AA reveal the membership remains overwhelmingly white (87%), with Latinos representing 5%, African Americans 4%, Native Americans and Asian Americans each 2% respectively. As White (2014) explains, AA's growth in other countries such as Mexico and Japan belie the criticism that AA appeals only to white males.

Regardless, it is impossible to overstate the impact of AA on alcoholism. AA provides much that is lacking in our modern culture – shared community; shared experience; shared spirituality – and may in fact be a harbinger of where society will move into the future. It continues to be a mainstay of addiction treatment, not only in the United States but across the globe.

## One Addict's Story

*The Cards Were Stacked Against Me*

> Each player must accept the cards life deals him or her: but once they are in hand, he or she alone must decide how to play the cards in order to win the game.
>
> Voltaire

I had a fairly stable childhood up until the age of 9. Seemingly stable. It was at that time that my mother and stepfather split up and I found out through my brother that my mother had a drug addiction – she free-based cocaine. So, we went from somewhat of an idyllic situation, a house on a cul-de-sac, a pool, the neighbor kids, to small, public housing, cockroach-infested apartments. It was a big shift.

There were suicide attempts, SWAT team raids, drug overdoses. My mom was a loving woman and a sick woman, and it was always kind of feast or famine. She'd have moments of trying to get her shit together, but it never lasted. She would cook her coke on the stove, in an omelet pan, and lock herself in her room. There was often no food, a lot of neglect. I remember a time when I knocked on her door because I was hungry; I was probably 10 or 11 at the time. She slipped $5 under the door so I could walk to the McDonalds and get my food.

I have a brother who is a few years older than me. So, he was with me through quite a bit of that. He himself developed an addiction. My mom had a boyfriend who actually shot my brother up with an IV needle for the first time; I was 14 years old when my mom first put pot in my Christmas stocking. This was an environment that was not only the norm, but it was condoned.

My grandparents, God bless them, were the strength in our family. Super conservative Christians and they send me to Christian schools. While my grandparents knew what was going on, and should have removed me from the home, they didn't. They hoped that going to the schools would make a difference, which I do look back on with gratitude. I was failing and missing a lot classes, so the school sent me to a drug-free youth conference where I met a man who I now know was someone giving a 12-step pitch. This was the first time I had heard stuff like that because we didn't talk about this stuff in my family. I told him what was going on, and he recognized the severity of it. He took me home and helped me to get into treatment. At that time, I was 16 years old. He came back, and he 12-stepped my mother and she went into the same treatment center, just on the adult side. And then after she completed that program, she went to sober living and put together some time in sobriety.

I did not. I wasn't done. I put together 30 days. I was the type of drug addict – certainly a bit depressed but I knew I was, pardon my language, "f****d" at a young age. I was addicted to meth and at one point, cocaine, and of course I drank too much but I was just always on something and it just got worse and worse. I started and stopped several colleges – always wanting to get my degree and never able to complete it due to my drug use and just general inability to function in life. I worked as a bartender at one point which I thought was the perfect job for me. I got my first DUI at the age of 24 and I got my second DUI 6 years later. About that time, my mom had relapsed, and I started taking opiate painkillers and benzodiazepines. I would go through cycles where I'd be super-addicted – couldn't function well on them, couldn't function off them and then I'd run out and go into severe withdrawals. I did not understand about addiction and alcoholism at that time. I just thought if I could stop the drugs then everything would be OK.

I'm not the type of alcoholic who lost everything, I'm the type of alcoholic who never gained anything. I was 33 years old when I got a phone call from my grandmother, that my mother had died of an overdose. It was both unexpected and expected. She was my mom and I loved her with all my heart. I was devastated. My brother by that time had two years sober. He had been in countless treatment centers, prison, and I saw him get sober. The day that my mom died, we went to her trailer where she died, and my solution was to go through the trailer and look for all the leftover pills that she didn't take because that's all I knew to do in order to cope with anything. I knew that I was exactly like my mom and I didn't want to be just like my mom, but I couldn't stop.

My drug use escalated to the point where I was probably taking on a daily basis the same amount that my mom used to kill herself. I would go to sleep at night and I would wonder if I was going to wake up because I knew what it could do but I didn't care. I wasn't overtly suicidal, but I was certainly apathetic. And then I'd wake up in the morning thinking about how I was going to get the stuff I needed. When I woke up in the morning with all the stuff I needed to get me through the day, that was as good as it got. My life had just gotten myopically small.

But there was one day when, as they say in the program, I had a moment of clarity when I realized that I didn't want to die, and I just couldn't get my shit together anymore. I knew I needed detox since I'd been in a couple of detoxes before, so I started calling around; I had no money, so I had to go to a state-funded place and you have to call every day before you get a bed. And then one day they said, "We have a bed. You can come at 1:00 and we'll do an intake and admit you." This was like 8 in the morning and I knew if I didn't go in right then that I was going to chicken out. So, I went and sat on those hard wood benches just shaking and it was there that I realized that it was two years to the day that my mom died. So actually, I share my sober anniversary with the anniversary of my mom's death. I have about 10 years, 9 months sober now.

In sobriety I didn't know what I wanted to do, and I had a really rad counselor in detox, so I decided that maybe I could work in recovery. And I thought I should get some sort of degree like I had always wanted. So, I earned my AA degree and got a certificate as a drug and alcohol counselor. I found out that I'm apparently quite smart and got an honors scholarship to a university and got my bachelor's degree and I literally just finished my comps for my masters in marital and family therapy. I'll walk with that degree. I'm thinking I'm going to go on for my PsyD.

I've worked in the field of addiction treatment since about one year of sobriety and now I'm the director of a treatment program. I've felt more at home in AA than in Nar-Anon because I just felt I was an alcoholic in the way that I did things. My brother had been in AA and I just followed his example. For me it was an emotional and spiritual component that needed to be addressed. I didn't come into the program knowing I was spiritually depleted, but I learned that through the process of the steps, the guidance of my sponsor, and others in AA.

I didn't have family support. I didn't have a mom and I didn't have a dad and my grandma was old and frail. But I did have a brother and it was kind of like we had been in a war together. He helped me by leaving me alone and just working his own program. You hear it in the program – attraction rather than promotion. He never said "You're an addict. You need help." He simply went from this man who couldn't stay out of prison or keep a needle out of his arm to a man who is successfully fathering his daughter, who is being of service to other people, who is flourishing in his career. The cards were truly stacked against him and me, and to watch him gave me hope that I could do it, too.

## Questions for Discussion

1. The text describes several common criticisms about AA such as "AA is just another form of addiction" or "AA is a cult." Are there others that you have heard? After reading this chapter, what is your perspective on this organization?
2. One criticism about AA has to do with the idea of admitting powerlessness. Some people see this as a way of avoiding responsibility. Others view this a form of passivity. What do you think about these criticisms?
3. Carl Jung asserted that alcoholism and addiction is a spiritual illness. This idea forms the crux of the AA model. How do you understand this assertion? Does this leave any room for those who don't believe in a divinity?
4. The disease model has been criticized over the years for various reasons. What might some of those reasons be? What is your view on this model?

# 4

# TREATMENT AS USUAL

## Current Model of Substance Use Disorder Treatment

> I did the program and moved into sober living and that was the first time I had followed the suggestion that a professional had made, and I think that was the difference. I was just willing to do whatever it took and just surrender and that was a big change for me.
>
> One Addict's Story

Interest in the nature and treatment of alcoholism and addiction has been long-standing in the United States, beginning with one of the founding fathers, Dr. Benjamin Rush. Since then the efforts to address this phenomenon have been numerous and varied. Currently, most treatment centers will follow some version of a model developed in the 1940s known as the Minnesota Model, named after the state in which this treatment was developed. This chapter will review the history of the Minnesota Model and its modern-day iteration.

## The Beginnings of the Minnesota Model

When researchers of addiction treatment refer to "treatment as usual," or TAU, they usually are referring to some variation of the Minnesota Model. As Lewis (2015) explains, "the Minnesota Model, which blended 12-step philosophy with principles of residential care and education, became the gold standard for treatment centers by the 1960s" (p. 14). The Minnesota Model evolved over the course of time beginning in the late 1800s when the Minnesota Board of Health called on the state to create an institution solely for the treatment of alcoholism (White, 2014, p. 261). Though request this was initially rejected, in 1907 the Minnesota legislature eventually voted to levy a 2% tax on liquor licenses to fund treatment centers. As a result, treatment centers began to multiply.

During the 1940s the AA program began to be incorporated into a residential treatment program called Pioneer House (White, 2014, p. 263). Shortly thereafter the now famous Hazelden center was founded in a Minnesota farmhouse with a focus on reaching male alcoholics who were still functioning with a job and family. Like Pioneer House, Hazelden was an early adopter of the 12-step model. By the early 1950s services were expanded to include a women's program.

A third program, Wilmar State Hospital, also contributed to the current Minnesota Model of treatment. Though initially focused on detox, administrators adopted the AA philosophy after observing the success of Pioneer House and Hazelden. In addition, they added some important components. First, the program would only address the problem of alcoholism, and not look for underlying emotional problems. Secondly, the program would include an emphasis on the spirituality. Thirdly, treatment would be delivered by a multidisciplinary team that included physicians, nurses, psychologists, social workers and clergy. In addition, recovered alcoholics were hired under a newly created position of Alcoholic Counselor (White, 2014, pp. 267–268).

The Wilmar program was centered on groups run by the Alcoholic Counselors and focused on exploring the experience of alcoholism while offering guidance and support for sobriety. This was in distinction to the psychotherapy groups run by psychologists which were aimed at uncovering the underlying causes of addiction. In addition to groups, the program included psychoeducation on the physical and psychological effects of alcoholism as well as the process of recovery (White, 2014, p. 270). Attendance at AA meetings was also expected, and meetings were held on the facility for that purpose. Patients were expected to organize and manage these meetings. In addition, the motivation for sobriety was assumed to be an outcome of treatment, and not a necessary precursor. This was contrary to prior assumptions that a patient had to be motivated in order to benefit from treatment. Finally, Wilmar began a formal aftercare program, following up with discharged patients and helping them to connect with AA members in their communities (White, 2014, p. 270).

During the 1960s Hazelden emerged as the dominant force of addiction treatment, eventually founding programs in other states and addressing the unique needs of individuals who may need more than the initial residential treatment. But the influence of the Minnesota Model has extended beyond these early developers so that some version of this model has been adopted by the majority of substance use disorder treatment centers.

## The Minnesota Model

White (2014) enumerates the general criteria of the Minnesota Model. They are as follows:

1. Alcoholism is an involuntary and progressive disease that, while not curable, can be arrested.
2. The motivation of the alcoholic at the beginning of treatment is not a predictor of treatment outcomes.
3. Treatment includes physical, social, and spiritual components.
4. Patients should be treated with dignity and respect.
5. The term "chemical dependency" best describes the problem, as alcoholics and addicts are typically susceptible to a wide range of mood-altering drugs.
6. Chemical dependency treatment is best undertaken by a multidisciplinary team who establish an individualized treatment plan for each patient.
7. Each patient is assigned a primary counselor, most often an individual of the same gender and in recovery from addiction.

8. The best treatment will incorporate the AA model and focus on working the 12 steps.
9. Treatment includes process groups, psychoeducation. and individual counseling.

As White (2014) explains, by the 1970s and 1980s "program staff who hadn't even heard of the Minnesota Model were following it" (p. 277). This underscores the tremendous influence this model continues to have on alcoholism and addiction treatment not only in the United States but in other parts of the world.

## The Growth of Substance Use Disorder Treatment

The 1960s saw the beginnings of dramatic growth in the number of addiction treatment programs. Some of this dovetailed with the professionalization of addiction counseling, the reinstitution of addiction medicine as a recognized specialty, and expanding coverage by third-party payers for addiction treatment programs (White, 2014). This, in turn, helped to destigmatize those individuals struggling with alcoholism and addiction and resulted in an increased public awareness of the AA model and the recovery movement.

While this has created greater access to treatment for most individuals, it has also brought with it an unfortunate emphasis on filling beds and a disincentive to track treatment outcomes, as doing so carries with it unwanted expense and the potential for a negative impact on admissions. For example, if treatment facility X decides to research the efficacy of their program and publishes their findings while other treatment facilities do not follow suit, then unless these findings are highly favorable, this can only have a negative impact on treatment facility X and a positive one for the other facilities who can claim recovery rates without having to prove them. This is, in fact, the situation currently. There are some treatment facilities that advertise recovery rates as high as 80% but without knowing the details it is impossible to verify this claim. As a result, it is very difficult to assess the average rate of recovery after a 30-day stay at an inpatient treatment facility.

In addition, treatment experiences are so varied – inpatient or outpatient; the length of treatment 30, 60 or 90 days; and aftercare programs and resources – that comparing outcomes for individuals who have completed treatment is further challenged. An individual completing a 90-day inpatient program, followed by 30 days in a partial hospitalization outpatient program, will likely have a different outcome than someone who participates in a 28-day inpatient program and then transitions into a sober living facility for the next six months. But that is a hypothesis that has yet to be proven. Add to this, one would have to consider the severity of the addiction or alcoholism; the interpersonal resources of the individual; and how the existence of a third-party payer may influence the treatment.

What we do know is that it is not unusual for an alcoholic or addict to have completed multiple treatment programs before stable sobriety is achieved and, sadly, for some this is never accomplished.

## Substance Use Disorder Treatment in the 21st Century

Treatment of addictions remains at the forefront of public concern, particularly considering the current opioid crisis. According to White (2014), on average, the cost of treatment per week in 2003 ranged from $700 per week for residential treatment, $462 per week for intensive outpatient treatment, the lowest being $91 a day for methadone maintenance (p. 424). In 2011, costs of private addiction treatment averaged around $25,000 for a 28-day inpatient program, with some more exclusive programs charging closer to $40,000. To put this cost into perspective, White (2014) notes that a cost-benefit analysis of addiction treatment reveals that for every $10,000 spent in treatment, society reaps measurable benefits in reduced societal costs of addiction (e.g., healthcare costs, job absenteeism/injuries, crime) ranging from $25,000 to $97,000.

Addiction treatment programs are required to be licensed by state agencies and more than half participate voluntarily in accreditation by external agencies, most notably The Joint Commission. The addiction treatment industry is represented by two major trade associations: the National Association of Addiction Treatment Providers and the American Association for the Treatment of Opioid Dependence (White, 2014, p. 425).

In addition, a phalanx of professionals provide treatment ranging from physicians who generally oversee detox, licensed mental health professionals like psychologists, marriage and family therapists, and social workers and addiction counselors who are usually certified by a national or state agency.

## Factors Influencing Efficacy of Treatment

The complexity of addiction is mirrored in the problems that treatment programs and professionals face when addressing the issue of effective interventions. So many variables affect the outcomes of treatment: length of time the individual has been an alcoholic or addict; the timing of entry into treatment; the length of treatment and subsequent aftercare; the age of the addict or alcoholic; and any concurrent mental disorders like depression, anxiety, or PTSD. For example, White (2014) reports that a 2012 national survey of drug use revealed that 23.1 million individuals over the age of 12 required addiction treatment but only approximately 10% of those individuals (2.5 million) received treatment. Those with an addiction to drugs were more likely to receive treatment than those who were dependent on alcohol (p. 432).

This highlights a conundrum in the addiction treatment profession concerning readiness to change or motivation. Most individuals in the above noted study (40%) reported that they were not ready to stop using. In the past, a truism held that an addict or alcoholic had to hit bottom in order to want to change but more recent studies have shown that individuals who are coerced into treatment, either by being placed in treatment as a minor by their parents or by a court mandate, have as good or better outcomes than those who come in voluntarily (White, 2014, p. 433). The problem is, as White (2014) points out, that mandated treatment usually comes at a late stage of addiction or alcoholism when the individual has already experienced a multitude of losses.

In addition, those who do enter treatment are unlikely to complete treatment or to remain sober, with 59% of those admitted to addiction treatment having had more than one prior treatment episode (p. 433). Treatment completion was achieved by only 44%

of those who were admitted to treatment according to a 2010 study reported by White (2014, p. 434). In general the recovery rate across all studies has remained around 50% though this data is difficult to verify with any accuracy. As White (2014) explains, nearly half of the individuals who do complete treatment will relapse within 90 days of discharge, with the highest percentage relapsing within seven days (p. 435).

## Further Research

Clearly addiction and alcoholism treatment is a complex problem. Much like cancer treatment, current research has revealed that the treatment should be more closely tailored to the individual rather than implementing a one-size-fits-all approach. White (2014) reports on a study conducted under the auspices of the National Institute on Alcohol Abuse and Addiction (NIAAA) which examines the idea of specialized treatment. Called Project MATCH, patients were randomly assigned to one of three treatments: 12-Step Facilitation; Cognitive-Behavior Therapy; or Motivational Enhancement Therapy. While the study, conducted in 1996, was not able to determine that matching treatment to an individual influenced outcomes, White (2014) notes that this led to increased increase in determining common factors that contribute to positive treatment results (p. 438).

In addition, improvements in brain imaging, particularly fMRI, have led to increased interest in neurobiology in general, and addiction in particular. While it is possible at this point to describe the brain functions that are most active in addiction, specifically those related to the dopamine system, and those that are less active, the higher-order systems related to long-term planning and delayed gratification, this understanding has not led to improvements in addiction treatment. This is due, in part, to the fact that these descriptions only underscore what is already known about addiction – that the desire for the drug of choice becomes all-consuming and that at some point almost all planning is focused on acquiring that drug. Other avenues have produced some medications, most notably naltrexone and acamprosate, to assist in treatment of alcoholism, and naloxone which is used in cases of opiate overdoses. At this juncture, however, there are no medications that address the root causes of addiction.

Various other models have emerged to address the multiple factors associated with alcoholism and addiction, including the developmental model of addiction, motivational interviewing, and harm reduction models. White (2014) categorizes the variety of philosophies that influence the addiction treatment profession as follows: 1. A medical model delivered by a physician; 2. A psychiatric model that views addiction as self-medication; 3. A psychological model that views addiction as maladaptive learning; 4. A sociocultural model that views addiction as a consequence of family dysfunction or peer socialization; 5. A spiritual model that views addiction as the failure of a search for meaning and purpose (pp. 465–466). The boundaries between the models are not distinct and most programs draw from several if not all of these models for treatment (p. 466).

What all of these approaches, both historically and in modern times, have in common is the emphasis on the treatment of the individual. This underscores the assumption that addiction and alcoholism are primarily problems of a particular individual – the addict or alcoholic – and ignores the alternative assumption that these are symptoms of a particular family system in which that individual is embedded. The latter perspective is much more difficult to grasp perhaps due to our cultural adherence to linear, cause-and-effect thinking and our emphasis on individualism. There is, however, a large school of thought that addresses general systems, and family systems in particular, concerning a myriad of challenges and issues. This is the topic which we will explore in our next chapter.

## One Family Member's Story

*Learning to Stand Firm and Let Go*

Courage is knowing what not to fear.

Plato

I'm an adult child of an alcoholic. I did not know this until I was about 14 years old when my parents separated, and my mom turned to wine in order to cope. I had no memory of either parent ever drinking throughout my life and was surprised to learn that when I was a baby until about 2 years old, both of my parents drank. My father was more of a social drinker, while my mother would have screwdrivers at home. One night, my parents left me home with a sitter and went out. My father told me he doesn't remember how he got home and was fearful something would happen where I would not have him in my life, so he decided to quit and hasn't had a drink in 30 years. My mother quit about a year later.

When my mom hit the bottle again, I was 14. My mother was verbally abusive, selfish and controlling in her alcoholism. My teenage years of finding myself, finding my confidence, and finding my friends was all put on hold while I tried to keep myself together as I never knew what kind of environment I was walking into. When I tried to live full-time with my father, she threatened to call the cops on him. One time in high school, I couldn't reach her and thought she had died. I was driven home in the middle of the day by the school police only to find her so passed out from drinking that she could barely move. I was ashamed. I had taken on her shame and made it my own. I was constantly walking on eggshells. Later on, I found myself in love with an alcoholic, thinking unconsciously I could fix him or be "good enough" for him to get sober since I felt I wasn't enough for my mom to get sober.

After years of this, and through my own therapy, I was finally able to set boundaries and not engage with her when she became abusive. I figured out what boundaries I needed to set by really recognizing how much emotional turmoil I was in constantly and recognizing when I felt hurt, sad, depressed. I struggled with setting boundaries initially because I felt guilty. I felt I was betraying my mom. I realized my trying to control how I interacted with her did not protect me since she wasn't respecting my initial boundaries so that's when I had to cut off completely. Some examples of boundaries that I set were – I'm not willing to have a relationship with you if you are drinking. I will not have a conversation with you if you have been drinking (text or otherwise). I will not answer texts or calls that are abusive in nature or threatening. Eventually, also that I would not see her anymore.

What helped me to stand firm was that I had an alternative safe place to go – my dad's (luckily, he lived a couple miles away). Looking back, I wish he would have protected me further, but he's told me that he never realized how bad it was for me. I also had the parents of my boyfriend at the time who I felt supported by. I was able to remember the importance of why I was setting boundaries because I could easily remember how painful it was to engage under chaotic circumstances. I was in therapy as a teenager during this time and was able to practice what I might say, and role-play possible reactions by my mother.

I became the "bad" one in the family for "abandoning" her, but really, I had been abandoning myself by allowing myself to be treated horribly. I stood strong knowing that I may never have a relationship with my mother again. One day, my mom called me crying saying she couldn't do it anymore and wanted to go to treatment. I spent the entire day calling places, only to find out once she sobered up, she had asked another family member to help and that person had already found a place and secured admission.

My mom went to treatment for 30 days. She has now been sober for about six years. But she is not in recovery. She stopped going to meetings the moment she walked out of treatment, she gave excuse after excuse why she didn't want to work with a sponsor. She is proud of her sobriety and makes sure to let me know on her birthday how long it has been. Not much has changed aside from the absence of alcohol; I now have my limited, emotionally unavailable mother back. I would take that over the drunk any day. Through my personal work, I can now have compassion for her limitations. I can accept her for who she is and let go of the mother I had always wished I had. And I can appreciate what she is able to give me, the gift and drive to help those who struggle with addiction as well as helping those live their best, authentic lives.

Some advice I would give family members who are going through this is be curious about why you want to set boundaries. If it is to try and threaten or manipulate the person into getting help, it won't, work – or it will but temporarily. You must do it for yourself and accept you are powerless. Addicts who have enablers take much longer to get help. Get support. Go to Al-Anon. Seek therapy.

One more piece to add: a couple years after my mom got sober, I wrote her a letter explaining how hurt I was about her asking me for help that morning when she decided she was done drinking then forgetting and asking someone else. She responded that she was drunk and did not remember even asking me, and apologized. If you (whoever the family member is) feel the need to bring up the past, be prepared for whatever response may come including denial of your reality, acknowledgment or anything in between. I waited a long time to send that letter because at first my intention was to get an apology. I needed to get to a place where I was expressing my hurt because it was what I needed to do to move on. It was just icing on the cake that she could acknowledge and apologize.

## Questions for Discussion

1. Current models of treatment tend to be based on the Minnesota Model. What are some of the characteristics and assumptions of this approach? What are some of its influences?
2. The chapter reviews the growth of SUD treatment since the 1960s. How do you account for this growth? What societal influences may be at work? What other factors may be influential?
3. The text explores the challenges in determining outcomes of treatment. What are some of the factors that contribute to this challenge? What impact does this have on treatment?
4. White (2014) argues for an approach to treatment that is tailored to the individual. What do you think the components of this would be? What would be the downsides?

# 5

# FAMILY THERAPY AND SUBSTANCE USE DISORDER TREATMENT

> My brother was 41 when he died. And it's interesting that to this day, my parents will say that he died of a heart attack. But because of my strong feelings about getting the word out in life, and I'm a straight shooter, I'll say "My brother's life was taken from addiction."
>
> One Family Member's Story

Even though family therapy has been a recognized approach to psychotherapy for decades, very little research has been done on its efficacy as applied to SUD treatment. This is particularly surprising given that the field of addiction treatment gives at least some acknowledgment of the need to include the family in treatment; yet the field continues to rely on individual therapy, most popularly CBT (cognitive behavioral therapy), and group therapy as the primary means to treat the disorder. This is in spite of the almost universal acknowledgment that addiction is a family disease. So while most addiction treatment facilities offer a family program, the focus of treatment remains on the individual. The NIDA identifies this as "family-informed" treatment. Typically, family-informed programs are composed of psychoeducation on the nature of addiction, some meetings with the family and the addict, and family activities. While these programs are helpful, they are not family therapy.

As we have seen, despite years of focused efforts on substance abuse treatment, relapse rates remain high. A consumer publication, *Drugs, Brains and Behavior: the Science of Addiction*, published by NIDA, reports the rate to be between 40% and 60% (NIDA, 2012, p. 26). This is compared to other chronic illnesses such as type 1 diabetes with a 30–50% relapse rate, hypertension with a 50–70% relapse rate, and asthma with a 50–70% relapse rate (p. 26). It should be noted that family systems theories see all of these illnesses as symptoms of a family disease with the most vulnerable individual in the family becoming symptomatic. From this perspective, it stands to reason the rates of relapse would be similarly high. But the medical community, as well as the field of psychotherapy, continues to place the focus of attention on the individual, ignoring the impact of the family system. This lack of understanding and lack of validation of the important role the family system plays is further evidenced by a list of treatments noted in the above-referenced NIDA publication wherein family therapy is at the bottom and then with the caveat "particularly for youth" (NIDA, 2012, p. 28).

Given the low rate of recovery after treatment for SUDs, it stands to reason that a revision of the current approach is warranted. There are some studies that have been conducted on family therapy in treatment for adolescents, however, which can offer some insights into the efficacy of this approach for adults.

## Brief Strategic Family Therapy (BSFT)

The use of family therapy in treatment for adolescent issues, including SUDs, is supported by research as an efficacious treatment, providing better outcomes than individual or group therapy alone. One example of this can be seen in research done using Brief Strategic Family Therapy (BSFT) by Horigian et al. (2015). This research evaluated the use of BSFT in affecting parental substance abuse as a means for decreasing adolescent substance use. Four hundred and eighty adolescents and their families were randomly assigned to either BSFT or Treatment as Usual (TAU) and assessed using several measures including the Addiction Severity Index-Lite and the Parenting Practices Questionnaire (Horigian et al., 2015, p. 45). BSFT integrates structural and strategic family therapy models to address systemic interaction, in this case relating to substance use. These include maladaptive family interactions, inappropriate family alliances, over-rigid or permeable boundaries and families' tendency to believe the problems are rooted in the individual (p. 46). The study found that BSFT had a positive impact on decreasing adolescent substance use. This was a result of a decrease in parental alcohol use, and an increase in family functioning (p. 48).

BSFT is also the topic of a manual for drug addiction published by NIDA (Szapocznik et al., 2003). The manual sites several studies that support the use of BSFT to treat adolescent drug use along with other co-occurring problem behaviors (p. 1). The goals of BSFT in this context are to eliminate or reduce the adolescent's use of drugs, and related behaviors, and to change the pattern of family interactions that are associated with drug use (p. 3). The authors provide an example of this by noting that parents' negativity toward the adolescent "directly affects his or her drug abuse, and the adolescent's drug abuse increases the parent's negativity" (p. 3). The goal of BSFT is to change this pattern of interaction to promote more positive family dynamics which will set the stage for a decrease in the adolescent's use of drugs.

Negativity in the family is a central characteristic of drug-abusing adolescents according to research cited by Szapocznik et al. (2003). In particular, this takes the form of family members blaming each other for the drug use, establishing a communication pattern that is chronically bitter, angry, and filled with animosity. Thus the goal is to reduce this negativity early in treatment, as research has demonstrated that doing so will increase the odds of the family remaining in therapy (p. 4).

Engaging the family in treatment is the focus of an entire chapter. Onc of the principal challenges lies in resistance to attending counseling sessions. This is due, in part, to the family members' tendency to see the problem in the addict and thus believe the addict is the only one who should be in treatment (Szapocznik et al., 2003, p. 43). As the authors note, "the families who most need counseling are those families whose patterns and habits interfere with their ability to get help for themselves" (p. 43). Viewed in this way treatment resistance is the result of the family's inability to adapt effectively to the situation and to collaborate to seek help.

The authors present clinical research supporting BSFT. In one study involving the treatment of conduct disorder, adolescents who participated in BSFT had an estimated 66% improvement while none of the adolescents in group counseling improved reliably (Szapocznik et al., 2003, p. 57). In another study which focused on marijuana use, BSFT was associated with significantly greater reductions in self-reported marijuana use than for those in enrolled in conventional group counseling (p. 57).

## Multidimensional Family Therapy (MDFT)

Another approach, Multidimensional Family Therapy (MDFT) was implemented in two studies on adolescents. The first, conducted by Hogue et al. (2006), focused on adolescent behavior problems, which included substance abuse. The emphasis was on the psychotherapy process itself with an examination of in-session client and therapist behaviors in order to understand and guide the efficacy of treatment. This study consisted of families who exhibited risk factors for adolescent behavior problems including parental disengagement, parental substance use, inadequate parenting practices, family conflict and distancing. These were predominantly single-parent households (53%), and African American (71%) families. Outcomes indicated that greater use of family-focused techniques during treatment resulted in a decrease in adolescents internalizing symptoms (anxiety, depression, and worry), an increase in family cohesion, and a decrease in family conflict which correlated with an improvement in adolescent functioning (p. 543).

The second study was conducted in 2014 as part of a European study of cannabis use among youth with co-occurring disorders. This study, the International CAnnabis Need for Treatment (INCANT), examined the effect of MDFT as compared to individual psychotherapy (IP) in both internalizing and externalizing symptoms in adolescents. Internalizing symptoms were defined as feeling anxious, worried, fearful, lonely, unloved, inferior. Externalizing symptoms were defined as arguing, aggression, stealing, and other behaviors in the conduct disorder spectrum. These behaviors were particularly correlated with substance abuse. Poor family functioning was also correlated with cannabis use and mental disorders. This study involved 450 adolescents between ages 13 and 18, over a period of 12 months. Therapists were trained in MDFT and received active supervision during the study. On average two MDFT sessions were conducted per week. Measures were used to assess cannabis use, internalizing and externalizing symptoms from both the adolescents' and parents' perspective, and the Family Environment Scale. The results showed that from intake to 12 months, both MDFT and IP performed similarly on outcomes measures. However, MDFT outperformed IP in reducing externalizing symptoms. The study also found that, contrary to popular belief among psychotherapists, adolescents who were "coerced" into treatment did as well as those who self-referred (Schaub et al., 2014).

## Bowen Family Systems Theory (BFST)

Finally, a study reviewing the application of Bowen Family Systems Theory (BFST) on chemical dependency was conducted by Cook in 2007. This consisted of a small sample of 36 chemically dependent men and women in outpatient settings who were interviewed to assess family patterns as identified by BFST. These included conflict, cutoff, sibling position, emotional triangles, the family emotional system, and the family projection process. Participants were randomly selected from a larger group of 120 for a structured interview and genogram construction. Their ages ranged from 22 to 55 years of age and ethnicities were primarily Caucasian and African American (p. 132).

Results indicated that conflict in the family of origin was the predominant characteristic of the family emotional system among the participants (Cook, 2007, p. 133). In addition, families exhibited a high degree of emotional cutoff from branches of the family, with many participants struggling to provide information about one side of their family system. This revealed a deficit in contact with that side of the family due to a variety reasons (p. 133).

An examination of sibling position revealed that the majority of participants were oldest, youngest or only children (62%), high risk positions for addiction. By far the most numerous were youngest siblings, followed by oldest with only a small percentage comprised of only children (Cook, 2007, p. 133). Along with sibling position, emotional triangles were identified most commonly as the participants feeling closer to their mothers and having neutral to negative experiences of their fathers (p. 133).

Finally, the multigenerational transmission of drug and alcohol abuse was clearly evident in the genogram constructions. Cook (2007) notes that "Persons completing the genogram interview repeatedly verbalized their surprise at discovering patterns of multigenerational transmission of conflict, communication patterns, and attitudes as well as incidences of chemically dependent people" (p. 136).

## A Developmental Model of the Alcoholic Family

Brown and Lewis (1999) offer insight into what they term the alcoholic family. Their research found that difficulties within the family remain after one or both parents have gotten sober and they have created a four-stage developmental model that addresses the issues the family faces during the recovery process. These include the Drinking stage, during which time most family members accommodate themselves to the alcoholic and generally are in denial about the negative effects of their loved one's drinking. The second stage is Transition, which emerges when family members begin to recognize that there is a problem that they are not able to control. This is the beginning of the process of acceptance and is highlighted by a willingness of family members to express themselves authentically.

The third stage in this model is Early Recovery. In this stage the alcoholic has entered recovery and is in close contact with 12-step programs. During this phase, the family members are encouraged to be engaged in meaningful activities which may include participation in family 12-step groups but also sports, hobbies, and other interests outside the family sphere. Finally, the family enters the Ongoing Recovery stage, during which time new patterns of interaction become the norm.

A review of literature reveals that research has focused on the efficacy of family therapy in the treatment of adolescent drug use. What are missing are clinical studies on the efficacy of family therapy on adult chemical addiction treatment. It can be inferred, however, that while there are some functional differences between adolescent and adult substance abusers, there are many similarities, chief of which is the idea that the influence of the family system remains throughout the life cycle of the individual. Focusing on this system as a means for change in the lives of one or more of its members is the hallmark of family system therapy.

## A Family Systems Approach to Substance Abuse Treatment

Part of the challenge in examining family therapy as an approach to addiction treatment lies in the philosophical differences between various theories. While there are many approaches to family therapy, two of the most prominent are Structural Family Therapy and BFST. While there are some areas of overlap, and even some common terminology, these two perspectives differ in case conceptualization and treatment methodology.

Structural Family Therapy was developed by Salvador Minuchin as an outgrowth of his work with inner-city families in Philadelphia. In common with other theories of family therapy, Structural Family Therapy sees mental, relational, and emotional challenges as symptoms of family functioning. Thus addiction in one or more family members is indicative of dysfunction within the structure of the family itself. Creating a functional family structure where roles, boundaries, and communication patterns are clear and appropriate is the goal of this approach (Minuchin et al., 2014).

The focus is on the nuclear family unit which is usually defined as those individuals residing in the household but can also include others such as adult children who have left home. The therapist will examine roles, hierarchy, coalitions, and relational patterns such as triangulation. Ideally the parental subsystem will work as a team to lead the family while the sibling subsystem will function as a coalition related to but separate from the parental unit. Communication lines will be clear and expectations appropriate to the developmental stage of the children. Problems arise when the boundaries between subsystems are either too rigid or too diffuse, communication is unclear, and coalitions exist between individuals in different subsystems (Minuchin et al., 2014).

The clinician's job is to both understand the existing structure of the family and unbalance it so that change can be made. To accomplish this the Structural Family Therapist uses a variety of techniques including challenging the family's certainty about the problem, in this case that the problem is the alcoholic. This might be done by exploring the idea that patterns of interaction between the family members could be contributing to the problem (Minuchin et al., 2014, p. 5). The therapist can also assist the family by exploring their existing relationship patterns through an enactment in the session that allows the therapist and the family to observe this process.

A different perspective is offered by Bowen Family Systems Theory (BFST) which was developed by Murray Bowen after years of working with schizophrenic populations at the Menninger Clinic and the National Institutes of Health. Bowen's experience with patients, who routinely decompensated after returning to live with their families, caused him to wonder if the focus of treatment was on the wrong person. Rather than focusing on the individual, in this case the one diagnosed with schizophrenia, perhaps the focus of treatment should be on the family system. From this, Bowen developed a comprehensive theory of psychotherapy that is systemic in perspective and thus a departure from the individualistic and linear approach that Western psychotherapy has long embraced (Bowen and Kerr, 1988).

Bowen's model, which is based on natural systems, holds that a change in one area of the system will result in a change in the entire system. For Bowen, the family system includes multiple generations in order to identify patterns that have recurred. And, while BFST would also see the addict or alcoholic as the symptom and anxiety-bearer for the family system, work is generally done with the individual who is in a position to make a change. This would be someone who is motivated to make changes and is autonomous. As Bowen (1986) explains:

> The therapy is directed at the family member, or members, with the most resourcefulness, who have the most potential for modifying his or her own functioning. When it is possible to modify the family relationship system, the alcoholic dysfunction is alleviated, even though the dysfunctional one may not have been part of the therapy. (p. 262)

BFST holds several key ideas. Foremost is the notion of differentiation of self, which can be defined as the ability to respond to an emotionally intense situation with thoughtful intention while at the same time having access to one's deepest feelings (Bowen, 1986, p. 362). This idea is frequently misunderstood as indifferent separation but that is a misreading of the theory. Reactive separation from the family system is indicative of a lack of differentiation because it reflects an inability to self-regulate when in contact with the family system. As Gilbert (1992) explains, "Highly differentiated persons have a superior ability to calm their emotional states, while the less differentiated person can be immobilized by emotion" (p. 24). Instead, differentiation is the ability to maintain regular, meaningful connection with the family system while at the same time holding onto one's principles and ideals.

BFST maintains that an individual's level of differentiation is roughly the same as the family system's since it is within the emotional environment of the family that a child learns to navigate important relationships. Thus an individual from a poorly differentiated family system will tend to have great difficulty in maintaining a sense of his or her self, being caught in what BFST calls emotional fusion. In families characterized by emotional fusion, the ability to process stress and anxiety is greatly compromised and the result is an increase in symptoms in the entire family system.

Differentiation underlies most of the other concepts of BFST. One way that this is identified is through the construction of a family diagram or genogram which gives a visual representation of family dynamics across generations. This multigenerational context is important because it is not possible to accurately identify patterns of relationships within the nuclear family alone. This is related to Bowen's concept of the family projection process in which the transfer of family anxiety, or emotional intensity, is passed along to the next generation, very often to the child most predisposed temperamentally to absorb it (Bowen, 1986, p. 384). An example of this can be seen in families struggling with addiction which exhibit this symptom across generations in one form or another. Usually, not every child in the family will become an addict, but the child who is most vulnerable as a result of physiology, temperament, and sibling position will be at the greatest risk.

Sibling position refers to the position an individual holds in the birth order of the family (Bowen, 1986, p. 384). As noted above, those who are youngest are at greatest risk for addiction, followed by firstborns. Those whose birth order places them in the middle of the sibling hierarchy generally have fewer symptoms, given that family anxiety can more easily be absorbed by either the oldest or youngest child. However, some families are so poorly differentiated and have such high levels of anxiety that all members may exhibit symptoms.

The emotional triangle is another key concept of BFST. Triangles are defined as a stabilizing process involving a dyad and a third person (Bowen,

1986, p. 372). As Gilbert (1992) elaborates, "Triangles are neither good nor bad. They just are, everywhere. As long as there is any undifferentiation left in the emotional system there will be triangles" (p. 81). Thus, learning to manage one's self in an emotional triangle is a key to differentiation.

When a dyad becomes unstable due to increased anxiety, a third person serves to diffuse the anxiety by taking the focus off the dyad. The most common triangle involves parents and a child in which one parent anxiously focuses on the child in an unconscious avoidance of conflict with their spouse. According to Bowen, triangles are a normal aspect of family functioning and it is only when they become rigid that symptoms will appear. A triangle often serves to freeze conflict in place so issues are never resolved but, instead, pushed aside in order to focus on the third person. In a family struggling with addiction, this would be exhibited as an anxious focus on the addict while other relationships are placed on the sidelines. Typically this looks like an isosceles triangle, in which the two closest members would be the mother and the child with the father in the outside position.

The final concept of BFST that is pertinent to this discussion is the existence of chronic conflict and emotional cutoff within the family system (Bowen, 1986, p. 382). These dynamics are somewhat interrelated since chronic unresolved emotional conflict often results in the decision to emotionally cut off by one or more family members. Gilbert (1992) explains this concept as follows:

> In fact, cutoff develops as an attempt to adapt to intense chronic and acute anxiety in the system. If we study the family system of one who is involved in cutoff relationships, we will usually find that there is more than just one instance of cutoff in the family. In fact, most often, many generations will have taken part in the same patterned response to intense feelings. It is only an end point in a long family emotional process.
>
> (p. 61)

In therapy sessions, this can be observed in a client who reports growing up with minimal to no contact with one side of his or her family. In addition, cutoff is evident when individuals claim that they have no family, which means that they do not know the members of their extended family. Sometimes this indicates that they were born into the branch of the family that was the most symptomatic. Bridging cutoff is part of the long-term strategy for assisting clients in lowering emotional reactivity and in raising their level of differentiation. This involves contacting a branch of the family that has been cut off and beginning to form meaningful relationships with those individuals.

## Bowen's View of Alcoholism in the Family

Bowen (1986) describes alcoholism as a symptom of the family system. The symptom, in turn, influences the other members in the family in such a way that the anxiety in the system is raised even further. He describes the process as follows:

> The symptom of excessive drinking occurs when family anxiety is high. The appearance of symptoms stirs even higher anxiety in those dependent on the one who drinks. The higher the anxiety, the more other family members react by anxiously doing more of what they are already doing. The process of drinking to relieve anxiety, and increased family anxiety in response to drinking can spiral into a functional collapse or the process can become a chronic pattern.
>
> (p. 259)

Bowen (1986) stresses the idea that clinicians should focus on observable facts – behavioral patterns, reactivity, etc. – and avoid trying to come up with causal explanations.

From Bowen's (1986) perspective, because it is an effective anxiety-binding mechanism in families, alcoholism is one of the common human dysfunctions that exist in the context of "an imbalance of functioning in the total family system" (p. 262). Thus, every important family member plays a part in maintaining this dysfunction. Therapy is aimed at assisting the family member or members to identify their contribution to this dysfunctional pattern without assuming blame, and then to develop some strategies for change.

Bowen (1986) identifies several clinical patterns that are evident in alcoholic family systems. One pattern involves an individual who is emotionally fused with their parents but reacts to this fusion by maintaining an exaggerated stance of independence. Often this person over-functions in their primary relationships until they become burdened by this stance and seeks relief by drinking (p. 264).

Another pattern occurs when the adaptive spouse, the spouse who is not an alcoholic, gives up his or her self in a form of emotional fusion. They react to their spouse's alcoholism by protecting both the alcoholic and the children from the problem. This is an attempt to avoid conflict but exacerbates the problems and the alcoholism, being a progressive disease, escalates.

Bowen (1986) acknowledges that alcoholism "is one of the most difficult of all emotional dysfunctions to modify regardless of the therapeutic problem" (p. 267). He explains that BFST does not offer a magic solution to this problem, but it does offer a different way to conceptualize the problem and to enhance the lives of the family members who come into treatment. He suggests several principles in working with families struggling with addiction/alcoholism.

1. Consider the degree of impairment in the alcoholic/addict. This would mean evaluating the personal resources and strengths of this individual, including his or her level of differentiation within the family system.
2. Examine the overall level of anxiety in the system. Those individuals who are most dependent on the alcoholic will be the most anxious about the problem. This, in turn, results in a higher level of criticism aimed at the alcoholic, who reacts by increasing his or her drinking, and thus the family system spirals into dysfunction.
3. Recognize that the alcoholic operates on a narrow margin between too much closeness (fusion) and too much emotional isolation (distance). Thus, a decrease in emotional isolation can result in improvement. It is possible to coach the family members to re-establish more meaningful contact with the alcoholic's parent family of origin.
4. Appreciate that if both spouses come into therapy the outcomes will be much more favorable. Even so, if only one spouse is willing to come into therapy, change is still possible. Sometimes the resistant spouse will eventually come in as well but regardless will be

positively impacted by the mature changes in important others (pp. 259–268).

## Conclusion

BFST is uniquely suited to work with families struggling with substance abuse because it does not rely on the participation of all members of a household or a nuclear family but rather holds that what is needed for change is one member who is motivated to focus on changing self. As Bowen and Kerr (1988) explains:

> Operationally, ideal family treatment begins when one can find a family leader with the course to define self, which is as invested in the welfare of the family as in self, who is neither angry nor dogmatic, whose energy goes to changing self rather than telling others what to do, who can know and respect the multiple options of others, who can modify self in response to the strengths of the group, and who is not influenced by the irresponsible opinions of others.
>
> (pp. 342–343)

Based on this assumption, one would predict the current poor outcomes of SUD treatment which focuses on the person who is in the poorest position to make a change. Addicts/alcoholics generally exhibit low levels of motivation to change and are not in a position of significant influence in their family system. Instead, the person in the most pain in the family would be the most motivated and thus in a better position to make use of therapy.

BFST holds that a decrease in anxiety in the system will result in a decrease in symptoms. Thus, if a mother of an adult alcoholic son, for example, decides to focus on changes she can make within her family system to more clearly define herself, her son will have a better chance of achieving and maintaining his sobriety. According to BFST, it takes only one person, maintaining a calm, non-anxious, meaningful presence, to change an entire system. It is this assumption that underscores the Family Matters program.

## One Family Member's Story

*Hindsight Is 20/20*

I have no desire to suffer twice, in reality and then in retrospect.
Sophocles

I was older than my brother by three years. We grew up in a divorced family. He was very introverted, a cute little blond boy, and kind of had a little eating disorder when he was around 10 or 11 and would only eat broccoli and stuff like that so he got really skinny. My mom was really anxious and a little neurotic. I got into partying, smoking pot and just doing all that social stuff when I was around 16 but my brother would come home from school and just go into his room. He never socialized. So, we just thought of him as like the straight arrow kid, but we found out later in life that at 11 years old, he was drinking in his room. It was shocking when he told me that because he was just the straightest arrow kid; he wouldn't party with us but when he was alone, he'd be drinking. At the time, I would never have guessed that.

We kind of grew apart and I moved to Oregon for a while. A cousin came to me one day and said, "I think your brother is drinking" and I was like "What?!!" I couldn't understand what she was saying, and I was in the addiction treatment field with teenagers! I was in total denial. I said something like, "You're crazy. There is no way. My brother does not drink" and I was very defensive. And it was very weird because I'm the one who is usually looking around every corner and doesn't believe anybody but when it came to my brother, I was just like "there's just no way."

During that time, my brother went into training to become a firefighter. My mother called me a few years later and said, "Mike is going into treatment for alcohol" and I was like, "Oh, my God! It's true!" So, he went to a rehab for alcohol and, at the time, I believed he got sober. I moved back to the area and I went to visit him one time, and I gave him a kiss on the cheek and I smelt alcohol. And I went, "No!" I lied to myself! I said, "No, I didn't smell it." It's just so weird how I removed myself in such an unusual way because I would be the first one to say "I smell alcohol" when I was at work.

My brother started dating a girl who was a nurse and he became a paramedic fireman. Looking back, I can see that his behavior was kind of weird. He would never socialize with me and he would fall asleep at movie theaters and stuff like that, but I never smelled alcohol on his breath again. But something kind of bugged me and I found out later that he was using pills then.

I introduced him to one of my best friends, who is the daughter of an alcoholic, so that was a relationship made in heaven. But I didn't know he was using drugs at all at this point. What happened was he broke his back on the job and was off work for six months and just got full-blown into pills. He was on fentanyl patches, and Vicodin; he was taking 30 a day. He actually got them from a local doctor who later went to prison for what he did to my brother.

The name of my story would be "hindsight is 20/20" because the whole time he was dating the other girl, I'd see my brother parked on the side of the road at like 6:30 in the morning or something and I'd think, "That is really odd". Then, once he was married to my friend, I started noticing that he had unaccounted time. Like I would be at my mom's house and then his wife would say, "Oh yeah, he was at your mom's house that day" and I'd say to myself, "No, he wasn't." So instead of my mind going to drugs and alcohol, because in my mind he was totally straight arrow, I thought, "Is he going to strip clubs?" You know, all these other things. But the whole time he was putting on his fireman outfit and doctor shopping. He got really bad. I can remember now, at lunches and holidays his eyes would be at half-mast. He was using.

I worked at a local treatment hospital and they gave my brother free treatment for two months. But a friend of mine, who was his counselor, would say to me, "As long as your brother works for the fire department, he's never going to get sober." Because he had access to all those pills as a paramedic fireman and the trauma, and all that. I've never even said this before, but for all those years, my brother volunteered for the cancer society and would bring people to their appointments and part of me says to myself, "Did he go so he could get their medication?" It's so painful just to say that. He was such a top-notch guy but there was this other side.

I remember at one point my dad saying, "You know, he looks a little tired" and I'm thinking, "You're in such denial!" At the end I took on a different persona. I was stressed and mad and telling his wife to leave him. I was so mad that my friends would tell me, after he passed away, that I would constantly say, "He's gonna die! He's gonna die!" And I don't remember ever saying that so when he died I was actually shocked. I was like, "What?!!" It's weird how I took on all the stress. I was the codependent right in the middle of it all, telling my parents how to deal with it, and blah, blah, blah.

One time we went to a family therapy session; we're in with 10 other families and we're all going around saying something. My mom says what she's going to say, and my Dad, who is an aerospace engineer and doesn't know anything about addiction, says, "I just want to tell you, I'm very disappointed in you!" And I remember just going, "Oh my God, that's the worst thing you could say." I just remember thinking, "No, Dad" but he was the kind that just thinks, you just don't do it. I remember asking my brother one time, "What is going on?" He says:

> I have so much shame, you don't know what it's like. You're mad at me because I don't just stop. I feel like I'm drowning, like I can't breathe. I've got this biggest hole in my chest and my stomach and all I have to do is put my hand on that life preserver over there and it will all go away. I just have to do it every time.

I just wasn't aware of the amount of shame he was feeling. In fact, one of my cousins who also was an alcoholic told me, "You just don't know how much shame he had. We have so much shame because of our addiction and you keep getting mad at him. We talk about it all the time because we feel so much shame." He never thought he was good-looking enough, good enough; he had all this going for him, but he was very hard on himself. I was just mad at him for what he was putting us all through that I didn't think about the shame.

My mom was such an addict; as a nurse, she would actually break into the office of the doctor she worked for to get the pills. She was always rattling around like a pill bottle when I was growing up. She was a functioning nurse/addict and every time something bad would happen and I'd come in crying, she'd say, "Take this!" and pop a Valium in my mouth. After my parents divorced, my mom married a man who was an alcoholic. He was a very fun, loving man, in fact my brother considered him his dad. And when my brother would stay with them, there was always a lot of alcohol in the house. One time when I came to visit him when he was 21 and in the fire department, I found ten vodka bottles under his bed and I was shocked!

One time, I had the idea to do an intervention. My mom, my dad, sister-in-law and I sat in the living room and my brother came home from work in the morning in his uniform and a pharmacy bag in his hand. We started to have this intervention and it was the worst thing we ever did. It was probably my idea since I worked in the field of addiction, thinking, "We can do this." And here's my dad thinking nothing's going on, here's my mom with her pills clanking around in her purse, here's me who's personally involved and my sister-in-law who's in denial and we're doing an intervention on my brother who just went doctor shopping! But unless they're ready, they're just not going to change.

When he passed away he had just gotten into trouble at the fire department. I don't know if he took medication from the unit or what, but he was on a leave, taking the fentanyl patches from the doctor, and he decided he was going to detox from them. He got Benadryl and Ativan and stopped using the patches and that's when he died, while he was detoxing. My brother's body could not handle the detox. My sister-in-law found him in the morning in the bathroom. She called me and told me something had happened to my brother and I'm thinking, "Here we go again" and I'm rolling my eyes, curling my hair, brushing my teeth, cause I'm in the pissed mode. I pulled up to his house and I saw the ambulance pulling away with nobody in it and I'm thinking, "That's a good sign." And I went up to the door and a fireman was at the door; I told him I was Mike's sister and he said "Well, I'm sorry to have to tell you but Mike passed away." I was shocked! You could have knocked me over with a feather because I had built this other scenario in my mind. Later they did this whole investigation into the doctor because they went into the medicine cabinet and found all these prescription bottles that had his name on them. It was in the newspapers in our area because this doctor and a pharmacist had just been handing out pills.

My brother was 41 when he died. And it's interesting that to this day, my parents will say that he died of a heart attack. But because of my strong feelings about getting the word out in life, and I'm a straight shooter, I'll say, "My brother's life was taken from addiction." It's really hard for me because I work in the field of addiction and I plead with the families, "Get into Al-Anon, anything, you need to understand what is going on. You are blind right now. You don't know anything!" I have a passion for the families given my experience with my brother. So, I reach out to the families and tell them, "You have to take care of yourself right now." I work in a high-end treatment center, I see more people dying than in other centers I've worked in with lower-income clients because of the opiates! And it's very sad – the high rate of relapse, the doctor shopping. I just say, "There but for the grace of God, go I!"

## Questions for Discussion

1. The focus of this chapter is on the use of family therapy in substance abuse treatment. How do you account for the lack of research on this therapeutic approach in substance abuse treatment?
2. The NIDA suggests that family therapy is an intervention best suited for adolescents. What are your thoughts about this assumption?
3. Brown and Lewis suggest a developmental model of the alcoholic family as it moves toward recovery. What are the stages of this model? How would this assist you in working with families struggling with addiction?
4. BFST is unique in its assumption that one motivated individual in an influential position can change the system. What implications does this have for working with families of addicts/alcoholics?

# 6

# THE FAMILY MATTERS PROGRAM

## A Program For families Struggling with Substance Use Disorder

> What do you first do when you learn to swim? You make mistakes, do you not? And what happens? You make other mistakes, and when you have made all the mistakes you possibly can without drowning – and some of them many times over – what do you find? That you can swim? Well – life is just the same as learning to swim!
>
> Alfred Adler

The family is the environment in which every human being grows and develops and this is not just the nuclear family or the family in the household, but the entire family system, stretching back generations. We come into this world only partially formed. We have innate temperaments and predispositions and a couple of instincts but beyond that we are molded by our environment; our brains are formed, the neuropathways developed, through the years of childhood (a particularly prolonged period as compared with other species). The debate is still ongoing regarding the role of nature versus nurture, yet we know with certainty that our brains are malleable. Thus, it makes sense to assume that the childhood environment in which a person's brain is formed would have an impress on their lives as adults.

Most adults have had the experience of going home to visit their parents for an extended period and finding themselves reverting to old behaviors. We think we have outgrown our childish selves only to find that, to the contrary, they have only lain dormant. Or we find ourselves in our relationships with our romantic partners arguing in the same ways in which we argued with our parents or siblings. We think that by leaving home, becoming an adult, finding a career, and creating our own families we have left behind our childhood selves, so it is very disconcerting to find that they have come along with us!

When it comes to our family systems, "Wherever you go, there they are" paraphrases a Buddhist aphorism. This encapsulates the assumptions of most theories of psychotherapy, especially family systems, that psychologically speaking, you carry your family with you. We intuitively know this to be true particularly when we consider the multitudes of family ancestors, most unknown, who came into and, through death, left the family with unique characteristics that have continued to live on in, us, their progeny. Thus, learning to change our reactions – change our established neuropathways – within the context of family relationships will result in lasting change. This will also create a change in the system and allow us to live more thoughtful, responsive lives.

## Pilot Program

The Family Matters Program was developed after a review of research studies I conducted in 2015 on programs that used family therapy to address the problems of alcoholism and addiction. Having worked in addiction treatment, I was aware of the focus on the individual during treatment and the adjunctive, and rather spartan, nature of family programs. Review revealed that research on family therapy and addiction treatment is limited. What little research exists has focused primarily on adolescents, with an emphasis on the use of either BSFT or MDFT as a treatment model.

Given the Bowen model's assumption that a change in one individual in the system will result in a change in the system I, together with my spouse and colleague, Ronald Bacon, created a pilot program to assess the validity of this assertion and to answer the question: if a family member makes a substantive change in their relationship patterns, will this increase the possibility that the addict or alcoholic will get into treatment and, if they are in treatment, will this increase the chance that this person will remain in recovery?

In response, we launched a small pilot 6-week program in 2016. Based on the ideas of BFST and Alcoholics Anonymous (AA), the program consisted of a 6-week series of two-hour workshops. Each session focused on different themes that were designed to assist family members in making changes in the family system.

The initial pilot was advertised via Facebook, email blast of the local chapter of California Association of Marriage and Family Therapists (CAMFT), Eventbrite, and word of mouth. Participants reserved a spot using Eventbrite. Two options were offered: a 6-week option held on Friday evenings and a 3-week option held on Sundays, with both programs offered to participants free of charge.

The pilot program enrolled 10 individuals who were family members of addicts or alcoholics. The demographic survey revealed that 50% of the participants were over the age of 50, and 100% of the participants identified as Caucasian. The majority (60%) had a high school education or some college while the rest had completed undergraduate education. Annual income ranged fairly evenly across the spectrum from $40,000 to over $150,000 with the largest percentage (30%) falling into the $40,000–$60,000 category. Seventy percent reported never having had any kind of psychotherapy. These demographics are likely indicative of the area of the county in which the pilot programs were conducted (Orange County, California), and the way participants were recruited.

In addition to the demographic survey, participants completed a Differentiation of Self Inventory – Short-Form (DSI-SF). The DSI-SF is a version of the DSI-R developed by Skowron and Friedlander in 1998 and revised by Skowron and Schmitt in 2003. The DSI-R is a 43-item self-report inventory containing four subscales: 1. Emotional Cutoff (EC); 2. Emotional Reactivity (ER); 3. Fusion with Others (FO); and 4. I-position (IP). Higher scores presumably correlate with higher levels of differentiation. Permission to use the scale was obtained from the author of the DSI directly (Skowron). Skowron and Friedlander (1998) reported internal consistency reliability estimates in an adult sample ranging from 0.74 for the FO subscale to 0.88 for the DSI full-scale score. Higher scores in the DSI have been correlated with lower levels of psychological symptoms and perceived stress (Murdock and Gore, 2004, p. 327). In addition, research has demonstrated that an increase in psychological distress is associated with an increase in perceived stress levels which in turn is more pronounced in individuals with lower levels of differentiation (p. 332).

Drake (2011) created a short-form version of the DSI-R selecting items from the DSI-R that demonstrated both significant information and discrimination between categories. The DSI-SF contains 20 items while retaining the four subscales of the original DSI-R (Drake, 2011, p. 49). As Drake (2011) notes, very little research has been conducted to support the use of the full-scale score but this is consistent with the definition of differentiation of self, according to BFST (p. 79). Drake recommends that caution be used with respect to "the moderate evidence of structural validity of the scale" (p. 82). He concludes by stating that the intention in developing this instrument is to assist in the promotion of well-being, which in turn will promote "the happiness of the individual and reduction of psychopathology" (p. 82). Thus, the utilization of the DSI-SF in this present study fits within the design and intention of the developers of both the DSI-R and DSI-SF instruments.

Of the 10 participants, two did not answer all the questions on the inventory. The reason for this is unclear but may be indicative of a lower level of differentiation as defined by BFST. The full-scale scores ranged from a low of 2.8 to a high of 4.05 with the average being 3.6. This indicates that most participants fell into the mid-range of differentiation in a range from 1 to 6.

Subscale results were as follows: Emotional Cutoff (EC), the average score was 4.18; Emotional Reactivity (ER), average score of 3.48; Fusion with Others (FO), average score of 4.34; and I-Position (IP), average score of 2.85. The latter was significantly lower than the others and may be indicative of difficulty in maintaining a clear sense of self and holding onto a thoughtful position while being pressured by others. This supports the intention of the Family Matters Program to assist individuals in gaining more clarity on themselves within relationship to others in the family.

Each participant was given a workbook summarizing the weekly themes and offering discussion questions and exercises to reinforce learning between sessions. The didactic portion of each session was supplemented by group discussion periods and brief film clips that demonstrated one or more of the weekly themes.

Engaging the family in regular attendance proved to be challenging. In the 3-week option, two of the four individuals only attended the first week, though the other two, parents of an addict, stayed for the full course. The 6-week group experienced similar results with most people dropping out after one session. Because of the small number of subjects (N=10) and the preliminary nature of the research, it was not possible to determine the reasons for the lack of retention, but some hypotheses can be made.

First is the absence of a fee. Generally, people do not value something they have not paid for, and tend to disparage goods and services that are low-cost. A second reason may have to do with the nature of families that have one or more family member struggling with addiction. The experience of the pilot program, albeit a very small sample size, was a mirror to that experienced by substance abuse treatment programs. From a family systems perspective, it would make sense that the family would exhibit the same types of resistance that the addict/alcoholic demonstrates in remaining in treatment. This has been noted by Szapocznik et al. (2003) who devoted an entire chapter to resistance in their manual on using BSFT in substance abuse treatment. According to this model, the principle of complementarity is at work, which means that the "behaviors of each family member must 'fit with' the behavior of every other family member. Thus, for each action in the family, there is a complementary action or reaction" (p. 49).

After conducting the workshop series, the two facilitators shared their suggestions for revising the program. Both agreed that the section on family diagrams (genograms) should be divided into more manageable subsections. Participants found the concept of emotional triangles to be the most easily understood, particularly when described in layman's terms. In addition, spending some time on the ideas of boundaries and roles within the family would be beneficial. Another refinement suggested including an elaboration on the various models of addiction.

The pilot program highlighted the need for some changes, and further research was conducted. Based on the feedback received from facilitators and participants, the following changes were made.

1. Revised the workbook
    a. Revised the family diagram section so that it is more easily understandable
    b. Highlighted emotional triangles and roles/boundaries in the first week
    c. Blended the AA portions into one section
    d. Addressed the issue of resistance in the first week
    e. Added a group process component

2. Utilized the Family Environment Scale (FES) instead of the Differentiation of Self Inventory (DSI).
    a. This is a widely used and validated self-report measure that measures patterns of interaction including cohesion and conflict. It is hypothesized that this will be a more effective means of assessing the efficacy of the Family Matters Program than the DSI which generally will not reflect change in such a short period of time.

## Revised Version

Between the initial pilot and the launch of the revised version, the opiate epidemic continued to grow nationwide. Although our original program was designed to be conducted in a traditional format, i.e., in person, we realized that this would greatly limit the accessibility of this program. With that in mind, we changed the format to an online course that would allow easier access to the materials and not be confined to a specific time and place. Since the Bowen model is a consulting or coaching model, this proved to be a good fit for this delivery method.

The basic program is divided into six modules, each of which is organized around a different principle of BFST and interspersed with information about the AA 12-step model. In addition, participants have the option to participate in one of two weekly video conferences to connect with other families facing similar challenges and to receive feedback from the instructors concerning strategies for change. In addition, questions and discussions are facilitated on a closed Facebook page – The Family Matters Community – to allow participants to share ideas, concerns, and other information with the facilitators and fellow students. The following is a review of the program, by module, and an examination of the ideas that inform each module.

## Module 1 – Introduction to a New Way of Thinking about Families

Assisting people to make lasting change involves a reorientation of default assumptions, beliefs, and behaviors. Every theory of psychotherapy touches on these three areas to a greater or lesser degree. How that is best accomplished is the ongoing debate in the field and the different theoretical approaches attest to these differences. As previously noted, the Bowen family systems model holds several key assumptions that underscore the Family Matters Program.

1. Members of a family system are interconnected, and this is not dependent upon the quality of the relationship or the proximity of family members.
2. A change in one area of functioning in a family system will result in a change in other areas.
3. It takes only one motivated family member who is in a position of influence, or is interested in holding an influential position within the family, to change the family system.
4. This is accomplished by thoughtful and strategic responses to relationship patterns that are typical in each family system. Specifically, the focus is identifying and changing the part one usually plays in these relationship patterns.
5. Since an individual's brain is formed within the family, lasting change is best accomplished by rewiring the brain within the context of that family system.
6. A shift in thinking about the family allows for ongoing improvement of functioning as it allows the individual to step back, or detach, from the family forces and observe the part each family member plays, including oneself. In so doing, the individual is then able to shift their reactions to thoughtful, intentional responses.
7. The goal of differentiation guides the process. Differentiation is defined as an individual's ability to experience deep emotions and

> maintain clear thinking while being in meaningful contact with the family. Alternately, it has also been defined as knowing when you're talking to someone else's brain stem.

Thus, a shift in perspective about one's family, consistent with an understanding of how one's family works, will help to create a more highly functioning family system.

### *Family Systems Assumption #1*

> All important people in the family unit play a part in the way family members function in relation to each other and in the way the symptom finally erupts.
>
> (Bowen, 1986, p. 259)

The first module is organized around the assumption that every person in the family influences other members and, in turn, the entire family system. Understanding this is crucial for individuals who have a loved one struggling with addiction because it begins the process of shifting the focus off the addict or alcoholic and onto the system, and more specifically one's own part in maintaining the relational patterns in that system.

Systems thinking is not natural for most people. We tend to default to a linear, cause and effect perspective. If there is a problem, we want to determine how to fix it and we generally assume that once we find the overt cause of the problem, we have found the solution. But this is not always a good model because often what we think is the cause is merely another symptom. For example, a homeowner discovers a water spot on his kitchen ceiling. He investigates and sees that a pipe in the upstairs bathroom has sprung a leak. So, he changes the pipe and assumes that has taken care of the problem. But a month later, he finds a leak in another area of the home. He calls an expert, a plumber, who informs him that the pipes in the entire home need to be replaced because the local water district has changed the composition of the water and this is causing pinhole leaks, not only in this person's home, but in houses throughout the area. A shift in one area of the system – the decision to change the chemicals in the water – initiates changes in the downstream plumbing.

This is something we experience regularly but for some reason we continue to assume that a more simplistic response to problems should be enough. We expect that if our addicted loved one would only get into treatment, the problem would be solved. Bowen's assumption is that unless the system changes or moves toward increased differentiation, the problem will shift to another area of the system. Without an increase in differentiation, even if the addict does achieve lasting sobriety, another member of the family system will become symptomatic. An example of this can be seen in the experience of a client who developed a problem with alcohol after his brother became sober from cocaine. The client, of course, did not connect these two experiences until we constructed his family diagram but then he was able to see this pattern quite clearly.

This lack of maintenance of systems thinking is partly because our reactions to the family system are not intentional and are largely unconscious. We are not aware of this influence because we tend to be so symptom-focused. Once we accept the fact that our family system influences us in ways of which we are not fully aware, we are better able to respond with conscious intention rather than unconscious reaction.

### *Wherever You Go, There They Are: Understanding the Power of the Family*

The Family Matters Program begins with an overview of the ideas of BFST which lays the foundation for the subsequent modules and allows the change in perspective that we believe is vital to a change in functioning. This overview, entitled "Wherever you go, there they are," begins with an explanation of the importance of understanding our family systems. We explore the challenges of relationships within families of origin and the opportunities these challenges present.

This section starts with a review of some of the key concepts that will assist in this process. The first is the idea that there are two opposing and equal emotional forces in family systems, and intrapsychically in individuals. The force of togetherness, the desire to affiliate with others, and the force of separateness or individuality, the desire to be able to express characteristics that make us unique.

## Togetherness-Separateness Continuum

These two forces form a continuum concerning managing conflict. Some families are closer on the togetherness end of the spectrum and thus tend toward what Bowen (1986) terms emotional fusion. Conflict is managed by impressing family members toward agreement and negating areas in which individuals might differ. These families will also manage conflict by having diffuse boundaries between individuals and by accusing those who have differing views of betraying the family.

On the other hand, those families on the separateness end of the spectrum manage conflict by distancing from one another. These families are low in affiliation. Contact between extended family members tends to be limited and communication more superficial. Each of these defaults – fusion or distance – has its unique set of challenges for the individuals who want to change themselves within their family systems.

## Differentiation of Self

The second concept is the foundational notion of BFST: differentiation of self. This concept is akin to cellular biology in which one cell will split off from an original cell but remain interconnected, even while this cell is distinct. This is how family systems can be viewed. In a highly differentiated family system, each member is connected to the others in much the same ways as the cells of a leaf are interconnected. The challenge with differentiation is related to the first premise – the forces of togetherness and separateness – primarily because being an authentic individual and staying in meaningful contact with one's family members is extremely challenging. Differentiation, and its corollary, authenticity, require a willingness to pay a price – at least in the short run. A person who stands on principle is challenged to conform to the family norm or pay the price for non-conformity. In some families, that price is very high. Only the person considering making a fundamental change can determine if they are willing to pay the price.

On a very basic level, this feels like a threat to survival. This is because our brains, having been hardwired in our family's emotional system, tend to react in predictable ways. This reactivity is related to the limbic system of the brain – the fight, flight, or freeze reactions, and has very little relation to the neocortex or thinking function of the brain. Differentiation of self requires an individual to lower the reactivity of the limbic system in order to have access to the neocortex. Doing so allows the individual to experience deeply felt emotions and at the same time maintain the capacity to think clearly and follow deeply held principles.

This is what Bowen (1986) calls the solid self. He explains:

> The solid self says, "This is who I am, what I believe, what I stand for, and what I will do or will not do" in a given situation. The solid self is made up of clearly defined beliefs, opinions, convictions and life principles.
>
> (p. 365).

This contrasts with the pseudo- or pretend-self which is composed of a variety of beliefs, ideas and principles that the group, or in this case the family, considers right or correct. These principles are acquired under pressure and, thus, according to Bowen (1986) are "random and inconsistent with one another, without the individual's being aware of the discrepancy" (p. 365). A main goal of the Family Matters Program is to assist participants in becoming more aware of his or her own deeply held values, and to act on those in relation to their addicted loved one, and other family members.

## Emotional Triangles

A third premise is that of emotional triangles. Because it is a lived experience, this concept is one that most clients understand easily. Emotional triangles are held to be the fundamental characteristic of relationships. Bowen believed that a dyad was inherently unstable, much like a two-legged stool, and that bringing in a third party stabilizes the relationship. As such, in BFST, triangles are not necessarily problematic. For example, if a marital relationship exists on the inside position of an isosceles triangle, with a child on the outside position, this will work for all concerned. The child will have the emotional freedom that being on the outside provides and the marital relationship will be functioning as a team. The same can be said for a couple working with a marriage counselor, provided the counselor is able to maintain a neutral stance, be on the outside position of the triangle, and not take sides. If the counselor does take sides, favoring one spouse over the other, then this counselor ceases to be a resource to the couple.

Emotional triangles are usually explored by starting with the primary triangle in an individual's life: the relationship with their parents. Asking who the person felt closer to as they were growing up reveals how this triangle was configured, and very often continues to be. For example, a person may disclose that they feel closest to their mother, experiencing their father as either distant or abusive. This person frequently feels protective of their mother and has difficulty seeing her part in maintaining the marital relationship patterns. In other words, they are unable to take a neutral position with their parents. Very often, this person feels pressured to support their mother and to help maintain their parents' marriage and this pressure results in an increase in anxiety, since on some level the person is aware that this is an impossible and unfair expectation. Identifying an active triangle allows the individual to change their position in the triangle should they decide to do so.

### Emotional Process in the Family

Finally, we present the idea of emotional process in the family. These processes, which are related to the concept of togetherness and separateness forces, are emotional fusion or reactive distancing. Fusion makes it difficult to maintain emotional equilibrium because the anxiety of other family members directly affects each individual, given that anxiety is highly contagious and easily transmitted. In other words, if one family member is in a state of high anxiety, the others will be similarly affected, and will react in an attempt to avoid or counteract the emotional intensity. This reactivity is lightning fast, and to family members seems to be second nature, but results in mindless patterns of interaction, such as overfunctioning-underfunctioning reciprocity, wherein one family member's underfunctioning results in overfunctioning by another family member. On the other hand, reactive distancing occurs when levels of conflict have remained high and one or more individuals emotionally disconnect, at least in the short run. The problem with both processes is that neither is based on thoughtful principle nor do these reactions result in any kind of long-term sustained change for the individuals or the system.

## Steps toward Differentiation of Self

The process of differentiation is often begun by constructing a family diagram, or genogram, a depiction of multiple generations of the family system that highlights emotional and relational patterns; identifying symptoms such as chronic illness, alcoholism, addiction, abuse, divorce, and affairs. When the family diagram is completed, it allows an individual to see the emotional patterns of the family system that have been passed down through the generations. This, in turn, enables the individual to see their family in a more neutral light and to identify ways in which they are perpetuating patterns that they may want to change.

Once this is done, there are a variety of options for the individual wanting to begin the process of change. These include:

1. Taking the energy invested in changing the other and focusing it onto self
2. Toning down the emotional intensity by observing the interaction, inhibiting one's own reactivity, and redirecting the energy
3. Shifting position in an emotional triangle
4. Connecting with challenging family members
5. Learning to approach others with curiosity instead of with an unstated agenda
6. Creating a life plan and moving forward toward personal goals

Once the person accepts the premise that their behavior influences the family system, then the next step is shifting the focus off the other family members, and onto oneself. This is accomplished by becoming aware of one's reactivity within the context of typical relational patterns. The Family Matters Program was created to start the process of change in this direction with the understanding that the participants will continue to work with a family therapist and a sponsor in Al-Anon or Nar-Anon.

## Working through the 12 Steps

Shifting the focus off the other person and putting it onto oneself is a very challenging concept. Most clients, for example, will give lip service to the idea that the only person they can change is themselves, but then proceed to spend most of the therapy session describing the behaviors of their loved one. One way to begin this process is to understand the idea of taking a position. Taking a position means that the individual has thought through the implications of a certain behavior or response and has decided to respond based on values or principles. This idea is introduced by reviewing one of the most difficult challenges of family members of addicts and alcoholics – what to do if that person will not get into treatment. In the Family Matters Program, if the participant is a parent, the suggestion is to start by not telling the addict what to do. Instead, the participant should determine what he or she will or won't do. If the addict is an adult living at home with a parent, the parent may decide that he or she is no longer willing to support addiction by offering free room and board. On the other hand, they may decide that they would prefer to continue to do that because they don't want to take the risk that the addict will come to some harm out on the streets. There is no right or wrong response; it is incumbent upon the individual to determine what position they are willing to take at the present time.

Taking a position requires a shift in focus but it also is aided by an understanding of what the family system has tended to do in similar situations over the generations. Thus, if a family has a history of supporting an underfunctioning family member, then making the decision to stop supporting that individual will be more difficult. This is because relationship patterns are transferred from one generation to the next, generally with increasing levels of intensity.

The changes that family members need to make will be very challenging. In fact, they mirror the changes that the addicted loved one will be facing in their recovery. To assist in taking the focus off the addict/alcoholic, the Family Matters Program introduces the principles of the 12-step family programs of Al-Anon and Nar-Anon. Understanding the principles of AA upon which all 12-step programs are based will assist family members not only in understanding the nature of addiction as defined by AA but also the challenges they face in learning to change their behaviors in relation to their addicted loved one. Over the course of the program, each step is reviewed with attention paid to how this step corresponds to the challenge of being in relationship with an addict or alcoholic. We encourage participants to investigate Al-Anon or Nar-Anon and to find a meeting that can serve as a resource for support and personal growth.

### *Powerlessness vs Acceptance*

> We admitted we were powerless over alcohol – that our lives had become unmanageable.
>
> Step 1 of the 12 steps of AA

Participants are introduced to the 12 steps of AA with an examination of the idea of powerlessness. This is a somewhat contentious notion that has been a focus of criticism over the years. Admitting that one is powerless does not fit the prevailing narrative of Western culture, particularly in the United States where independence and self-efficacy is venerated, even if it is not always practiced. But the fact is that everyone has faced situations in which they were powerless. This is not to ascribe powerlessness in every situation; nor does it exonerate the alcoholic or addict from responsibility for managing their addiction. As is clearly seen in subsequent steps, part of moving toward a spiritual awakening, i.e., finding serenity and peace, requires taking responsibility for the harm one has caused while in the grip of addiction and, when it is possible, making amends for the damage.

While the first step in the 12 steps of AA is admitting powerlessness over alcohol, this is a principle that can be applied to any behavior that a person has tried to stop without success. All of us have experienced a person, event, situation that we cannot change, and learning acceptance is the first step toward emotional freedom. It is easy to see the unmanageability of the alcoholic's or addict's life; it is harder to see it in ourselves when we think we look so controlled by comparison. Step one is the beginning of a spiritual journey and many religious traditions hold to this concept – that we must come to the end of what we know how to do to be open to change. Accepting that one is powerless is not the same as passivity or weakness; it takes a great deal of strength and courage to admit we are powerless. It wounds our pride but that is what is known in religious traditions as a sacred wound. It is a necessary wound if we are going to deepen our experience of ourselves and others.

For the family member, the first step is admitting they are powerless over the alcoholism or addiction of a loved one. Paradoxically, this allows those family members to be empowered to change what they can – themselves. This insight is underscored by theologian Reinhold Niebuhr, who wrote the Serenity Prayer, the first part of which is repeated at 12-step meetings worldwide:

> God grant me the serenity to accept the things I cannot change;
> the courage to change the things I can;
> and the wisdom to know the difference.

When the family member shifts the focus off their addicted loved one, and puts it onto themselves, they will be empowered to make the changes necessary to move closer toward a life of serenity and peace. And much as life improves immensely for alcoholics and addicts once they stop drinking and using, it's more difficult than it appears.

## Module 2 – Choosing Life

Family members usually don't realize how much they have organized their lives around the addiction of their loved one. People report changing jobs to keep a closer eye on the alcoholic or constantly checking to see if their addicted loved one has used their drug of choice – "Are his eyes dilated? Does he have that 'look' on his face that he gets when he's stoned?" Sometimes the addiction seems to invade every aspect of family life so that what is most distinctive about the family is the addiction. This module moves the process of self-focus forward by exploring another important principle of BFST.

### *Family Systems Assumption #2*

> The part each person plays comes about by each being him or herself.
>
> (Bowen, 1986, p. 259)

This module is based on a second assumption held by Bowen that the individual's normal or natural way of being is contributing to the maintenance of patterns of interaction. Thus, change involves becoming counterintuitive, going against what feels right and natural, and responding to situations based on thoughtful intention.

An example of this can be seen in the following scenario. A mother whose son is addicted to meth knows that he will call her as soon as he runs out of money and beg her to give him some cash. He usually threatens her with some dire consequence if she doesn't – "If you don't give me the money I need, someone is going to kill me!" Or he may cry, "I don't know where I'm going to sleep tonight!" Her normal reaction is to act out of fear and anxiety and give him the money. On some level she knows this is probably not a good idea, but she is too frightened to consider something else and she hopes that each time will be the last time. In order to change this pattern, she decides to prepare in advance for this phone call. She makes a list of possible responses:

1. She could continue to give him the money
2. She could give him a prepaid credit card
3. She could take him out for a meal if he is hungry
4. She could buy him groceries
5. She could offer to take him to a treatment center

She thinks about these options and quickly rules out the first because this is what she has always done. The second is better but a prepaid credit card can be traded for drugs. She decides that she will combine options four and five. She will offer to buy him groceries and offer to take him to a treatment center.

Now she plans what she will do when he calls. She knows that he will not be happy with anything other than her giving him money. He will get angry, threaten, and yell to get her to back down. She will need to hold her ground and calmly repeat "I am willing to buy you some groceries and take you to a treatment center for help." If he escalates, she can always hang up the phone. She is also prepared to do this multiple times over the next few months. She is doing this, not to get him to change, but to change herself. She is also doing this to bring her behavior in line with her values. She does not believe in supporting his addiction but that is what she does when she gives her son money. She believes in supporting recovery and that is what she will do.

She also has an Al-Anon sponsor whom she can call if it becomes too difficult. She can attend an extra meeting to get additional support. Eventually, this will become the new normal and she will have made an important change in herself. Instead of just "being herself" she is learning to be a new self.

This challenging process usually requires the assistance of a trained psychotherapist and we highly recommend that participants seek out this resource. In addition, the Family Matters Program offers a weekly video conference option during which participants can receive consultation from the facilitators. Participants can also post questions on the closed Family Matters Community Facebook page which is moderated by trained facilitators.

Changing one's self is a lifelong process, but it does not require a 180-degree turnaround. Small changes in responses to others in the family can have large results. For example, making the decision to stop participating in pointless arguments will decrease frustration and animosity almost immediately. Making a subsequent decision to approach the other person with curiosity, and without an unstated agenda, would have an even greater and longer lasting effect.

BFST also recognizes that not only the individuals involved in the dyadic interchange (i.e., the mother and her addicted son) will be affected, but so will the family system. Thus, the mother may receive negative comments from others in the family. Some may argue that anything she does for her son is co-dependent; she should just use tough love and not talk to him until he gets into treatment. Others might urge her to give him money and point out that if her son's life is truly being threatened, she would feel terrible if he did end up dying. Both responses are an unconscious change-back reaction from the family system and are predictable. The family system resists change, even change for the better, and members of the system will act to bring individuals back into their pre-existing patterns of behavior. But this change-back reaction does not last and eventually the new behavior will become the new normal.

## Taking a Position vs Giving an Ultimatum

The concept of taking a position, determining what one will or will not due based on a value or principle, is different from telling the other person what they should do and then delivering an ultimatum if they do not comply. Taking a position is not other-focused; it does not depend upon the other person's response. Taking a position is self-focused; ideally it is solely dependent upon one's own intention to operate out of principle. Thus, the anxious energy that was focused on the loved one will be withdrawn, leaving that addict or alcoholic with less of a countervailing force to act against.

An example of this would be a woman who is married to an alcoholic. Over the years she has cajoled, pleaded, and threatened her husband to try to get him to stop drinking alcohol. She has delivered ultimatums such as "If you don't get into treatment, I'm going to leave you" but has never followed through on her threat. This time, however, she decides to take a position based on principles. She is clear that she is tired of letting alcohol run her life. She is also aware that she has allowed this to be the case by hoping that she could convince her husband to get into recovery. Now she considers her alternatives:

1. She could stop threatening to leave. This would be an improvement if she does not intend to leave since it would align her behaviors with her inner reality.
2. She could start attending Al-Anon meetings and focus on her own program. This would start the process of shifting her focus from her husband to herself.
3. She could decide to move out of the house. She could tell her husband that she will no longer allow alcohol to run her life. If he chooses to get into treatment and recovery, she would be willing to remain in the household. But if he decides that he'd prefer to keep things as they are and continue drinking, she will move out.

He is likely to hear this last option as an ultimatum. "Now you're just telling me what to do," he might say. Her response would be, "No. You are free to drink alcohol as much as you want. I am talking about me, not you; I am not going to live with someone who is an alcoholic." She would need to be sure that this is a position she is willing to take. If not, she can start with the first two options. Those would be a change in the right direction and a movement toward differentiation of self.

This kind of strategizing requires awareness of one's principles and values. In the Family Matters Program, we ask the participants to take a values inventory to help them identify their top five values; this underscores the importance of introspection and self-awareness in this process.

### *Constructing a Family Diagram or Genogram*

To assist in identifying the multigenerational relationship patterns of their family system, participants construct a family diagram. This visual depiction of family dynamics across generations allows the participant to appreciate the larger context of their own lives, not only the challenges but also the strengths that they have received from being a member of this family. Though the family diagram resembles a genealogical chart, the emphasis is on patterns of interaction, with various symbols denoting conflict, fusion, cutoff, as well as psychological and social symptoms such as mental illness, alcoholism, addiction, and marital affairs. Deaths are noted, including the date and the age of the individual as well as the reason. In short, this is a comprehensive depiction of a family system through multiple generations.

Though this will be an ongoing process of discovery, the initial diagram can reveal a great deal, even with minimal information. For participants in the Family Matters Program, constructing a family diagram assists in taking a systems view of the problem of addiction by shifting the focus off the alcoholic or addict and seeing them as part of a larger whole. This serves to lower the emotional intensity directed at the addicted loved one and will allow for greater emotional freedom for both the addict and the family member.

### *Embracing Pain for Greater Good: Steps 2 and 3 of the 12 Steps*

> Came to believe that a Power greater than ourselves could restore us to sanity.
>
> Step 2 of the 12 steps

> Made a decision to turn our will and our lives over to the care of God as we understood God.
>
> Step 3 of the 12 steps

Most spiritual traditions encourage acceptance and surrender as part of the road to peace and transformation. Step 2 follows the acceptance of powerlessness on the part of the addict and step 3 builds upon this by turning one's will over to the care of God, or a Higher Power. Some addicts will argue that they do not believe in a Higher Power when, in fact, their drug of choice has been their higher power. We encourage our participants to appreciate the spiritual nature of the journey to recovery. And, most importantly, to realize that this is true of them as much as it is their addicted loved one.

In addition to recommending that participants join Al-Anon or Nar-Anon, we suggest the time-honored traditions of meditation and contemplative prayer. Sitting quietly each day and observing one's thoughts and feelings without judgment allows the participant to restore equilibrium so that the limbic system of the brain is less easily activated. This enables the participant to respond with greater acceptance of their life's circumstances.

Acceptance, in turn, predisposes the participant to grant themselves and others a measure of grace. This can be challenging because people tend to believe that unless they are hard on themselves, they won't accomplish anything or will become selfish and narcissistic. This belief underlies the perfectionism that is so prevalent in those struggling with addiction. In fact, the opposite is true; those who can give grace to themselves are more likely to be able to accept feedback and change their behaviors and be willing to grant others grace in return.

## Module 3 – A Wide Angle Lens

This module is the halfway mark of the Family Matters Program. Thus far participants have been introduced to some of the ideas of BFST and the principles and philosophy of AA and the 12-step movement. In this module, participants continue to build on this foundation with an introduction of the concept of emotional triangles and how to change one's part in this pattern.

### *Family Systems Assumption #3*

> The symptom of excessive drinking occurs when family anxiety is high.
>
> (Bowen, 1986, p. 259)

When Bowen uses the term "family anxiety," he means the overall level of emotional intensity. When it is elevated, it is as though the family exists on high alert all the time – even when no overt threat exists. Individuals who are raised in this environment will have greater difficulty responding to normal challenges of daily living with clear thinking and intention. Individuals whose family systems are more differentiated, and thus experience lower chronic anxiety, will be able to adapt more successfully to changes and stressors in the family and the environment

The term anxiety does not refer to the diagnostic category of anxiety disorders. For Bowen, anxiety is defined as a tendency toward reactivity (as opposed to being responsive) and difficulty in maintaining clear thinking. When emotions run high, maintaining a level of thoughtful reasoning becomes very challenging, even under the best of circumstances, and when a family system exists at a level of high chronic anxiety, this makes clear thinking almost impossible.

This idea is related to Bowen's use of the term reactivity. Reactivity is a reflexive response to a perceived threat that bypasses the cognitive levels of the neocortex. An example of this can be seen when an individual is driving a car and another driver makes an unexpected lane change. A reaction to this on the part of the first driver might be to slow down, honk the horn, or swerve to avoid a collision. None of these reactions is the result of careful, thoughtful intention. There is no time for that! This is helpful during times of imminent threat but for some families, this type of reactivity is normal and expected.

In families where there is a high, chronic level of anxiety, members tend to struggle. Alcoholism and addiction are two symptoms that can emerge when a family system is in constant red alert. The good news is that it takes only one motivated individual to change a family system. A calm, non-anxious presence can lower the levels of anxiety in any situation.

### *Emotional Triangles and Common Relationship Patterns*

Emotional triangles are an important concept of BFST. Bowen held that a two-person relational system, or dyad, is inherently unstable and requires a third person to provide stability. Thus, for Bowen, triangles are not necessarily problematic. However, very often triangles that are chronic and unbalanced, i.e., not equally sided, contribute to the symptoms the family is experiencing. Bowen held that triangles emerge out of the separateness-togetherness continuum that is inherent in every family system and within every individual. We want to be a part of something, to feel as though we belong (together), and at the same time we want to be uniquely individual (separate). In a dyad, the person who has the most discomfort will move away from the other person and toward a third party. This will reduce the intensity in the dyad but increase anxiety in the third person. A common triangle is that of a married couple, the dyad, and a child, the third party. This is not a problem if the couple can work through conflict and keep the energy between the two of them. However, most of the time this is not the case. The intensity between the couple results in one of them shifting focus onto a child. This contributes to symptoms in the child and thus reinforces the need to focus on the child at the expense of the marital dyad. The problem with an emotional triangle is that it freezes conflict in place. This explains one of the reasons why the divorce rate at around 20–25 years of marriage is so high. Children have usually left home and now the couple is faced with years of unresolved conflict.

While this is the most common triangle, there are many others that can be just as intense and can be simultaneously active. For example, the wedding gift triangle is very common, usually consisting of a husband, a wife and the husband's mother. In this case, the triangle is the result of unresolved conflict between the husband and his mother which he psychologically transfers to his wife. The husband is in the outside position of the triangle as the wife takes up the conflict with her mother-in-law. This gives the husband a feeling of emotional freedom from the conflict, but it also prevents him from accomplishing an important psychological task and, in turn, is likely to create conflict with his wife.

In addition, there are several relationship patterns that contribute to the intensity of relationships and usually result an emotional triangle. These are: the pursuer-distancer dynamic; the overfunctioning-underfunctioning reciprocity; and conflict-cutoff. Each of these patterns is the result of reactivity on the part of each individual. In the pursuer-distancer dynamic, the pursuer seeks increased connection but does so in an anxious way, very often with anger. The distancer, seeking to cool things down and lower the intensity, will withdraw either physically or emotionally. The more the distancer withdraws, the more intensely the pursuer pursues.

The second pattern, the overfunctioner-underfunctioner dynamic, occurs when one partner becomes anxious more quickly than the other and responds with increased activity. The husband may become anxious about the amount of pet hair on the carpet and react by vacuuming more often. His overfunctioning in this area, perhaps vacuuming daily, will result in his wife's underfunctioning in this area. Usually the overfunctioner assumes the other person is not pulling their weight while the underfunctioner believes their partner is being unreasonable.

Finally, the third pattern, conflict-cutoff, occurs when levels of conflict are chronically elevated, resulting in one or both parties cutting off contact, at least for a period. The problem with this pattern is that the conflict does not lead to resolution, creating a pattern of conflict followed by emotional cutoff. This is a pattern that, in a married couple, frequently results in divorce.

Triangles emerge to lower the intensity of these patterns. To step into a less reactive, more functional position, an individual must first identify which part in the pattern he or she is playing and then strategize a response that is in keeping with their values and principles. In families struggling with addiction, this will often involve the relationship with the addict. The overfunctioning-underfunctioning reciprocity is a very common pattern in such families, with one person, perhaps a parent, overfunctioning to try to save their addicted child from the negative effects of addiction. This usually results in creating an environment which actually prolongs that addiction. Taking a position is particularly challenging if the addicted child also has children. Families with this situation are frequently in chaos as the addiction or alcoholism becomes the focal point of the family, and anxiety overwhelms the family. Stepping out of the overfunctioning position is particularly challenging and requires that the individual access various resources of support, including an Al-Anon or Nar-Anon sponsor and a trained psychotherapist.

Whatever the most predominant relationship pattern, once an individual recognizes their part in maintaining the pattern, they can move to restore self-focus and lower the intensity not only for themselves but other family members.

### *Self-Examination: Steps 4 and 5 of the 12 Steps*

> Made a searching and fearless moral inventory of ourselves.
>
> Step 4 of the 12 steps

> Admitted to God, to ourselves and to another human being the exact nature of our wrongs.
>
> Step 5 of the 12 steps

Steps 4 and 5 of the 12 steps are reviewed in this next section of Module 3. These two steps are linked together; step 4 is incomplete without step 5, and step 5 only has meaning considering step 4. Step 4, making a "searching and fearless" moral inventory, has its roots in the spiritual tradition of confession. The old saying "confession is good for the soul" applies here. Taking the opportunity to review one's life and examine the impact of poor decisions can be both painful and liberating. For the addict, this means focusing on how they have wounded other people while they were in the throes of their addiction. For those who don't struggle with chemical addictions, a moral inventory means reviewing how they may have hurt others, intentionally or not. For families of addicts, this could include admitting to behaviors that have allowed the addict to continue to use.

Making an inventory and then admitting to the nature of those moral failures is a difficult undertaking. It is likely to bring about feelings of shame, one of the most painful human emotions. To counteract this, it is important to approach this exercise with self-compassion and acceptance of one's humanity, understanding that to be human is to be flawed. It is important to know that having failed at something does not make a person a failure. Perfection is not the goal of the 12 steps, nor should it be the goal of any spiritual practice. As a favorite saying of AA states, "Progress not perfection."

For family members, conducting a searching and fearless moral inventory will set the stage for the serenity and peace that can be experienced as a result of working the 12 steps. These steps allow the individual to be released from the burden of past moral failures. They also result in a greater capacity for empathy and compassion for others.

## Module 4 – Shifting Focus

The next module in the Family Matters Program continues to build on the ideas of BFST by assisting participants in shifting focus off the addicted loved one. This module starts with an exploration of another important assumption of family systems thinking.

### *Family Systems Assumption #4*

> The appearance of the symptom stirs even higher anxiety in those dependent on the one who drinks.
>
> (Bowen, 1986, p. 259)

As you may recall, in BFST, anxiety refers to chronic levels of threat. Anxiety in this sense is contagious, particularly when it is escalating. This is evidenced in the way in which panic can create a reaction in a crowd of people that is very powerful and even life-threatening. When the group begins to run in one direction, survival would depend on the individual to determine (a) if running in that direction is an appropriate response and (b) if the group is headed in the right direction.

This is similar to the way in which family systems behave. It is common to react without thinking through the possibilities in times of threat. Learning to settle down the anxiety and access the thinking part of the brain requires practice. This is particularly challenging when an individual is financially dependent. This situation is often the case in couples in which one partner is an alcoholic or addict but is the person who is the major breadwinner. However, dependence can take many forms. Simply loving someone deeply can result in a feeling of dependence since anything that threatens that relationship will naturally raise anxiety levels. If that person is struggling with alcoholism or addiction, then an increase in use by addict will result in an increase in anxiety in the family member.

While this is understandable and, in fact, is to be expected, high levels of anxiety make it difficult to determine how to respond effectively. And even if an individual does know how to respond, anxiety can impede following through on that knowledge. An example of this would be a father who continues to bail his addicted daughter out of jail, even though he knows that doing so will contribute to her continued addiction. His anxiety about her well-being is so high that it overrides his thoughtful intention.

To counteract this, we suggest that participants identify their typical reactions to repetitive challenging interpersonal situations. They start by making a list of these situations and identifing the typical physiological and behavioral reactions, such as distancing from others or becoming irritable. Once this list is completed, the next step is to come up with alternate responses based on values and principles. Participants are also encouraged to practice approaching their addicted loved one with curiosity, asking good questions (i.e., questions for which one does not already have an answer), and seeking to understand rather than change the other person. This is in itself represents a significant change and it will also facilitate meaningful contact and decrease anxious focus, another step toward differentiation.

### *Emotional Freedom: Steps 6 and 7 of the 12 Steps*

> Were ready to have God remove all these defects of character.
>
> Step 6 of the 12 steps

> Humbly asked God to remove our shortcomings.
>
> Step 7 of the 12 steps

The famous photographer Ansel Adams had a saying, "chance favors the prepared mind." Adams was renowned for his photography and was known to wait days for just the right light. Anything worth having is worth waiting for is another pertinent aphorism. The 12 steps are meant to be completed in order because one step typically builds on the one before. In this case, step 6 builds on the preparation done in steps 4 and 5. It also underscores a paradox, which is that an individual needs to lay the groundwork in order to be ready to receive grace. The definition of grace is unmerited favor. In other words, grace is not something that is earned or deserved and yet for grace to be received one needs to be receptive. The 12 steps of AA state that that each person must make a searching and fearless moral inventory (step 4) and confess this to themselves, others and one's Higher Power (step 5); this, in turn, prepares the individual to be ready to have God remove the defects of character (step 6).

This leads to step 7 which states that the person must "humbly ask" God to remove these shortcomings. Only a Higher Power, the God of each individual's understanding, can transmute character defects into character strengths. For addicts, these two steps continue the process of moving toward Spirit and away from spirits (drug of choice). This why AA is firmly rooted in the notion of a spiritual awakening. Those who have been in the program long enough have a character of true humility become more compassionate human beings. This is one outward sign of an inward journey.

## Module 5 – Investing in Sobriety

This module focuses on the idea of investment – not just of money, but of time, energy and commitment. What we choose to invest in should be the result of conscious intention but all too often that is not the case. For example, many of us find ourselves spending a lot of time doing things that are really not that important to us. We may start the day with an intention to spend time on what is important only to find, at the end of the day, we never got around to it.

Moreover, unless we have already identified what we are willing to invest in, we won't have clear guidelines when we are presented with a decision. Our family members can frequently bring us to this point and unless we have prepared ahead of time, or at least determined not to make a decision until we have had time to think it through, we will default to reacting. This usually means we will find ourselves investing in something we don't really believe in.

This module is aimed at helping the participant avoid this pitfall and be prepared for the challenges, not only with their addicted loved one, but of life in general. Knowing one's deeply held principles and values is the first step. Having resources to help the individual hold onto a position based on those values is another important tool.

In addition, Module 5 reviews the fifth assumption of BFST and offers suggestions for bridging emotional cutoffs, developing communication skills, building trust, and moving forward in steps 8 and 9 of the 12 steps of AA.

### *Family Systems Assumption #5*

> The higher the anxiety, the more other family members react by anxiously doing more of what they are already doing.
>
> (Bowen, 1986, p. 259)

Anxiety, and more to the point, anxiety management, is an overarching concern of BFST. The anxiety in the family system can be mitigated by the thoughtful responses of one individual of influence in the family. Bowen distinguishes between reactivity or reactive actions, which are generally a regression and an expression of immaturity, and responsive actions, which are based on thoughtful intention. An example of this can be seen when someone is speaking to another person who doesn't speak the same language. Often that person will speak more slowly, and more loudly, as though this will assist the other in understanding. In relationships, this phenomenon is evidenced by one person speaking more loudly, and more insistently, to get the other to understand (best translated as "do what I want"). In either case, speaking more insistently, loudly, or slowly does not work. In the second example, a responsive action might include lowering the tone of voice, becoming curious about the other person to better understand their thinking, and asking questions that will help clarify. One common reaction to intensity in the family system is seen in the relationship pattern of conflict and cutoff.

### *Conflict and Cutoffs*

Regardless of how a family system manages intensity, all family systems will experience some degree of emotional cutoff, an outcome of a lack of differentiation. Emotional cutoff is a discontinuation of contact with another family member or members. As Bowen (1986) explains:

> The more intense the cutoff from the past, the more likely the individual is to have an exaggerated version of his parental family problem in his own marriage, and the more likely his own children are to do a more intense cutoff with him in the next generation
> (p. 384).

Emotional cutoffs, therefore, are perpetuated across generations. The problem with cutoffs is that they do not allow for a resolution of the conflict and leave family members with a lack of skills in effectively managing conflict in subsequent generations. Changing this pattern requires re-establishing meaningful contact with members or branches of the family of origin that have been cut off in order to move toward a higher level of differentiation.

The most common example of a cutoff is divorce but estrangements between a parent and child, or siblings, are also common. Initially, cutoffs seem to reduce tensions in a family as the opportunity for conflict is eliminated. But in the long run, emotional intensity is pushed down into the next generation, causing problems that seem unrelated to the cutoff but which are, in fact, a direct outcome. This can be seen in the example of a single mother who decides to cut off from her parents and siblings because she considers them to be "toxic." She moves to another state, taking her two children with her. Because she is no longer in contact with her extended family, she lacks the resources that families frequently provide during times of trouble. She struggles to provide for herself and her children and lives on the edge of financial catastrophe. As her children enter their teen years, she experiences greater conflict with them. In fact, she has replicated the same relationship dynamic with her older daughter that she had with her own mother. Because she and her children are isolated from their extended family, the emotional intensity is much greater. Eventually her older daughter runs away from home and thereby repeats the pattern of conflict and cutoff that her mother experienced. This is how cutoffs affect generations, not by some overt means but by reducing the family system's ability to successfully manage conflict.

One way to understand how cutoff contributes to emotional intensity is to imagine five people living on a small island. Because there are no other outlets for relationships, these individuals will experience much greater conflict and intensity with each other. Being connected to a larger family system allows the emotional intensity to be spread across a larger number of people. It also allows for support during times of challenge – illness, unemployment, bankruptcy. The greater the numbers of family members who are in meaningful contact with each other, the greater the level of potential support for the individual.

One symptom of emotional intensity, and cutoff, is addiction. Addiction serves to put the focus on one individual – the addict – and as a result, other areas of potential conflict are ignored. It is not uncommon for the other members of an addict's family to appear to be higher-functioning while the addict is in an active addiction. If there are no changes in the family system, however, once the addict becomes sober, the addict will either relapse or some other member will become symptomatic.

Bridging cutoffs can help to settle down the intensity in a family system. It is as though energy that has been bound up in maintaining the cutoff (as in "we don't talk to those people" or "your grandfather left his family but would never speak about them") is now free to enliven the individuals in the family, creating less intensity and greater ability to think clearly in response to stress.

In the Family Matters Program, participants learn to review their family system and patterns of interaction, including cutoffs, and then determine a strategy for changing their typical patterns of interaction. We recommend that people start with a family member who is challenging but not too difficult and then work up from there to the more difficult relationships. This serves two purposes: 1. It will take the focus off the addict/alcoholic and 2. It will eventually result in fewer symptoms in the participant.

### *It's Not Communication if No One Is Listening!*

Good communication plays an important role in lowering emotional intensity but all too often the focus is on talking rather than listening, convincing rather than understanding. The best way to circumvent this tendency is to approach family members with curiosity. The goal is to become a non-anxious presence in the family system, particularly in relationship with the addicted loved one. When an individual is non-anxious, or calm, they can think clearly, ask good questions, and truly connect with another human being. Thus, the first step in clear communication is to take the focus off the fears, anxieties, and other concerns and instead, become curious as to the other person's thinking.

The next step is to schedule a time to talk, or more importantly, to explore and listen to the other person. The goal is not to get this person to change but rather to assist in changing self. One five-minute talk in which an individual is truly listening is golden.

This leads to the third step, which is to set a time limit. This is particularly true when the topic is emotionally charged. The emotional brain is the elephant upon which the thinking brain is riding; thus, it is important to be realistic with how much time can be spent in a discussion before becoming overwhelmed with emotions. This is why participants are encouraged to shift their focus onto themselves. They need to be aware when they are becoming anxious or defensive or angry. Once this occurs, it's time to shift to another topic or do something else – take a walk together, watch a movie – anything other than continue the conversation. The fourth step is to realize that this process is not about problem solving. It is about learning and understanding. It is also not about agreement. It is possible to understand someone else without agreeing with them. That is a hallmark of empathy. And yet, this is very difficult! This is one reason why individuals tend to have repetitive arguments over and over again.

An individual can change their part in this pattern by deciding to start off by being the one who listens, not only by asking good questions but also by reflecting back what they heard the person say. This is not simply parroting, but stating in one's own words the essence of what was heard. "So what I heard you say is that you think you should have the car even though your license is suspended." Here's how this conversation might continue:

| | |
|---|---|
| YOUR LOVED ONE: | "Yeah. That's what I said. So can I have the car?" |
| YOU: | "No. But I certainly understand that you would like it." |

| | |
|---|---|
| LOVED ONE: | "What?!! But I need that car. I can't go to work without a car! Why are you punishing me?" |
| YOU: | "You think I'm punishing you by not giving you the car?" |
| LOVED ONE: | "Yeah. You're being unfair. Now I'm feeling like I want to use again." |
| YOU: | "What do you think you can do about that?" |
| LOVED ONE: | "I could use again." |
| YOU: | "Anything else?" |
| LOVED ONE: | "Call my sponsor." |
| YOU: | "Well, I'd certainly prefer that option but as you know it's totally up to you." |

### *Amends: a Willingness to Repair and Renew: Steps 8 and 9 of the 12 Steps*

> Made a list of all persons we had harmed and became willing to make amends to them all.
>
> Step 8 of the 12 steps

> Made direct amends to such people wherever possible, except when to do so would injure them or others.
>
> Step 9 of the 12 steps

The Navajo have a philosophy called "hozho" which encompasses the idea of beauty through order and balance. When someone has wounded another person, this creates a state of imbalance in that individual's personal and social worlds. Unless that person asks for forgiveness from those they have hurt and does something (make an amend) to restore that balance, they will never be fully in harmony with themselves and others.

This idea is reflected in the eighth and ninth steps of the 12 steps of AA. It is a recognition of the toxicity of guilt and remorse that can be remediated only by some sort of action. It begins with making a list of those who have been harmed by that individual. For an addict or alcoholic, this list will reflect the destructive aspect of their disease. For the Al-Anon or Nar-anon member, it might include the hurts caused by an over-focus on the addict to other family members or to the addict themselves. Once this list is reviewed, the next step is to make direct amends, except when to do so would cause harm to others. This last injunction is important because sometimes revealing how one has injured another person may do more harm than good. But these two steps are more about freeing the individual then receiving forgiveness. In fact, if that is the goal, the individual is likely to be disappointed. Sometimes the harm that was done is too grievous to be forgiven, or the other person may not be ready to extend forgiveness. This is to be expected and accepted if one, to use an AA aphorism, accepts life on life's terms.

Notice, too, that the individual needs to become willing to make amends. This can be a process and is best undertaken with the understanding that making amends is aligning one's behavior with one's values. This dovetails nicely with the idea of differentiation found in BFST and is one reason why the Family Matters Program sees these two – BFST and AA – as working in tandem. Thus, in making amends the focus should be on learning to be more fully integrated with one's principles and values. This makes an individual less vulnerable to the responses of others in seeking forgiveness and in making amends.

What constitutes an amend will depend on many factors, but it could involve writing a letter, making a visit, giving a meaningful gift, or making an apology. I recently worked with a client who had 10 years of sobriety from methamphetamines. He reported that when he was in the throes of his addiction, he had stolen money from his young son's piggy bank to buy drugs. He was feeling tremendously remorseful and guilty. I suggested that he estimate how much money he had stolen, add the appropriate amount of yearly interest to that sum, and then pay his son back. This would allow him to restore harmony to that relationship and to release him from the burden of guilt by making an amend. He followed through on this suggestion and later reported that this had marked an important milestone in his sobriety and his relationship with his son.

## Module 6: Moving Forward

This final module is designed to recap some of the important ideas explored in the program and to assist participants in making plans to continue the process in the future. In addition, Module 6 reviews the final assumption of BFST that applies to this program as well as the last two steps of the 12 steps.

### *Family Systems Assumption #6*

> The process of drinking to relieve anxiety, and increased family anxiety in response to drinking, can spiral into a functional collapse or the process can become a chronic pattern.
>
> (Bowen, 1986, p. 259)

Bowen had an early interest in families struggling with alcoholism. Though he was asked by the National Institute of Mental Health (NIMH) to head up a program to focus on treatment of schizophrenia, his ideas concerning both disorders were the same; mental illness or addiction are both symptoms of anxiety in the family system. According to Bowen, the most vulnerable member of the family will become the most symptomatic.

This vulnerability may be due to this individual's predisposition to the symptom, or it may be a result of other factors such as temperament or birth order.

What Bowen means by functional collapse is the squandering of the family legacy – business, real estate, reputation, social connections. To prevent these losses, a family member will step up to forestall a calamity by relying on their default responses to threats. Usually the person who reacts first to these threats will be an overfunctioner and often the person closest to the addict or alcoholic. An example of this is a wife who routinely calls her husband's workplace to report that he is ill when, in fact, he has a hangover after a night of drinking. It is understandable that she would do so, given the threat to the family's livelihood. However, in so doing, she is mitigating the pain of her husband's alcoholism and prolonging the addiction. She may do this because this was how this type of threat was handled in her family of origin or she may be responding to a threat in a way she has done habitually.

To change this would require that the wife find the courage to define self and become as interested in the long-term welfare of the family as in her short-term well-being. She would work to respond without anger or dogmatism, but rather with her values and principles. This means that her energy will go, not to changing others, in this case her alcoholic husband, but to changing herself. She might stop calling his work for him or covering up his alcoholism in other ways. Next, she would decide what she will do if he persists in his alcoholism. She would take the time to consider each of her options and weigh them against her values and principles.

Bowen firmly believed that when one family member moves toward differentiation, the family symptoms disappear. This person would be the de facto family leader. Not because he or she is in a position of power but rather due to their influence. Thus, as Bowen also states, a responsible family leader automatically generates mature leadership qualities in other family members who are to follow (Bowen and Kerr, 1988, pp. 342–343.)

### *Mindfulness and Thoughtful Intention*

Lowering reactivity is an important component in moving toward serenity and peace. Though being less reactive is an admirable goal, it is a particularly challenging one. In this section, participants are introduced to the insights of neuropsychology in order to assist them in accomplishing this goal. The discussion begins with an overview of brain functioning with an emphasis on the limbic system as the seat of emotions. The limbic system is the largest part of the brain and is responsible for the flight-fight-freeze response. Hanson (2013) points out that the human brain is like Velcro for negative experiences and Teflon for positive. This is because positive experiences are less likely to affect the limbic system since there is no threat involved. In order for a positive experience to stick to the brain and have an affect it needs to be exaggerated. Hanson (2013) recommends a process for actively reversing this polarity by attending to positive experiences and expanding them emotionally. He uses the acronym HEAL to describe this process: Have a positive experience; Enrich it by attending to it and allowing yourself to be aware of how wonderful it feels; Absorb it by allowing this experience and the good feelings to sink into conscious awareness; Link it to negative thoughts and experiences in order to help heal those painful memories. This approach can be employed regularly to lower chronic reactivity.

### *Meditation and Prayer: Helping Others – Steps 10, 11 and 12 of the 12 Steps*

> Continued to take personal inventory and when we were wrong, promptly admitted it.
>
> Step 10 of the 12 Steps

> Sought through prayer and meditation to improve our contact with God, as we understood, praying only for knowledge of God's will for us and the power to carry that out.
>
> Step 11 of the 12 Steps

> Having had a spiritual awakening as a result of these steps, we tried to carry this message to alcoholics and to practice these principles in all our affairs.
>
> Step 12 of the 12 Steps

These last three steps bring the individual to the summation of a spiritual journey, continuing the practices of self-reflection and self-evaluation, seeking God's or one's Higher Power's guidance and, in turn, carrying this message to others who need the help AA can give. The twelfth step also highlights the need to practice these principles in all areas of life, not to compartmentalize these principles to only one aspect. An example of this is the concept of rigorous honesty. For an alcoholic, this means that to maintain sobriety the alcoholic or addict must be willing to admit when he or she is thinking about drinking or using, preferably to their sponsor. They must also be willing to be honest about their behaviors, their intentions, their plans. This is because addiction is so intertwined with lying and dishonesty about even the most trivial matters, that if someone in recovery lies that is considered the beginning of a relapse.

As step 10 emphasizes, it is vitally important to continue the practice of reviewing one's life and making amends. This is part of what assists an individual in connecting with God or a Higher Power, to one's inner life and with fellow human beings. Step 10 reinforces the previous steps and sets the stage for the final two. As Rohr (2011) explains, "Whenever we do anything stupid, cruel, evil or destructive to ourselves or others, we are at that moment unconscious" (p. 91). In other words, step 10 is about maintaining awareness in order to be most fully ourselves.

Step 11 switches the focus to prayer and meditation, what is most commonly known as contemplative prayer. This form of prayer is different from other types of prayer in that rather than focusing on speaking to God, contemplative prayer is concerned with listening to God, with being aware of God's presence in that moment. One form of contemplative prayer is called "centering prayer." This involves sitting quietly, focusing on a word or a phrase that is meaningful such as "peace" or "love". When thoughts, worries, or concerns pop up, simply observe them and let them go. This is a form of mindfulness meditation that allows the individual to be aware of thoughts and feelings without acting on them.

Step 12 has to do with giving back out of gratitude. In AA, this means giving of one's time and attention, perhaps serving as a sponsor, and to the greater community. Step 12 is an outcome of living a life of integrity and authenticity or, in the words of AA, "walking the talk." A word that fits this principle is "praxis" – praxis means that one's behavior matches one's stated beliefs or values. Thus the twelfth step integrates all the other steps that have come before it into the intention to live out the philosophy of the 12 steps in one's daily life.

## Conclusion

This chapter has provided an overview of the Family Matters Program, with emphasis on the guiding principles found in BFST and the 12 steps of AA. These two programs work in tandem to assist the participant in shifting the focus off the addicted loved one and onto self. From the BFST view, this represents movement toward differentiation of self within one's family system by allowing principles and values to guide behaviors. Though AA holds as its goal a spiritual awakening, which is viewed as an antidote to the power of alcoholism and addiction, this too is a process that assists the participant in maintaining self-focus and acting on principle. The 12-step program gives form and substance to an otherwise ephemeral concept of spiritual awakening with the goal of experiencing serenity and peace even in the midst of the challenges of life.

## One Addict's Story

*Where Do I Belong?*

> That is part of the beauty of all literature. You discover that your longings are universal longings, that you're not lonely and isolated from anyone. You belong.
>
> F. Scott Fitzgerald

I had the beautiful, perfect all-American family ... as far as everyone else was concerned. Of course, that wasn't true. Dad was a gunnery sergeant in the USMC; Mom was a stay-at-home mom until we moved when I was about 7 and she started working for my uncle. That made me a latchkey kid. I had two older brothers; three years older and seven years older – I was the baby and the only girl. I was always a disappointment being the only girl because I wasn't girly. My oldest brother started drinking in the home when he was 16 because they were of that mindset. Dad had gambling; Mom had food. Dad also smoked but they didn't drink and do drugs so as far as they were concerned there weren't any problems. My Dad's mom was a full-blown alcoholic and an exotic dancer, so my dad was exposed to a lot of inappropriate sexual experience at a young age; he was also a victim of sexual abuse, so, no boundaries.

At age 7, I started smoking Dad's cigarettes; by 9 I had started having a little bit of alcohol here and there. My brothers and I would throw parties on Saturday nights when Mom and Dad were gone. By the time I was 11, I was a full-blown alcoholic and I was sleeping with my brother's friends. My pay-off was a 4-pack of wine coolers outside my bedroom window.

I was 12 the first time I tried meth. I had already tried marijuana from my younger brother's friends. I don't really remember the first time I tried meth because it was so mixed in with everything else. In my mid-teens, I wound up with a guy who was 20 years old and in the navy. Eventually, the story of my abuse came out.

I was at a slumber party at the house of one of my best friends and I was caught by her at the side of the house making out with one of the boys. I didn't know she had a crush on this boy. She basically called me an F***n slut. And I don't know where it came from – down from the depths of my soul – I started crying and I said to her, "If you were raised like I was, you would be too." And she started crying because she had also been victimized. So, she knew exactly what I was talking about. Her mom wanted to talk to my mom, but another mother called social services and the police showed up at my junior high; they talked to me and my friend. They eventually ended up taking us down to the police station and I started out by telling them about my brother, and then a cousin, and I wound up telling them about my dad, who was my primary abuser. It was very embarrassing to be taken in the back of a police car in front of everyone at my junior high. But I had been living this lie since I was 4 so I didn't really know about the difference between good touch and bad touch. There was never any threatening – it was not violent. I just worked really hard to protect my family image and I felt like I had just screwed that up. It was my job to protect the family, that's just how I thought.

That day, my dad was off work and supposed to take my mom out for lunch and he found out that I was taken down to the police station. My dad's response was, "Do me a favor and make sure my car gets home" and he drove down to the police station. I heard my dad come into the police station. He said, "You have my daughter here. Everything she said to you is true. Please let her go home with her mom." He wanted it over.

Of course, they didn't let me go home with Mom because she was charged with not protecting me. She didn't have a clue even though my grandmother had mentioned things to her in the past. Anyway, they took me out of the home and sent me to Orangewood, a county facility for kids that traumatized me even more. I was then put in foster care, which was another bad situation. The foster mother resented the fact that my mother called me every day, and tried to make me feel bad about that, because the other kids' moms weren't calling regularly. But even at that age, I knew that I didn't have anything to feel guilty about. She decided not to keep me and so the social worker told me I had to go back to

Orangewood. I told her, "No. I'm not going back there and if I do, I will run away." So eventually my grandmother took me in.

Meanwhile, my brother was fully into his meth addiction and we already had a family therapist. So, we all did a lot of therapy – a lot of therapy! I got involved in Daughters and Families United; I spoke to victim's groups. Dad was sentenced to six months. I still couldn't go home because my brothers still lived there. And that's how I came to live with Grandma and Grandpa.

That summer I went to a camp for children who had been victims of abuse and while that was rough, that was when I figured out I was a lesbian. I fell in love with a camp counselor. She didn't know and no one else knew and I sure as hell didn't know what was going on. I was 15 at the time. I was engaged to that navy guy. It was very scary. I had been accused of being gay my whole life and I'd get threatened at school. But I was a fighter though mainly I fought in defense of others. That's when my drinking took off – full-blown. Isolation and self-punishment for being everything negative that people thought I was. Plus, all the other stuff. I came home from that camp and the very next day, my fiancé came over and I told him, "I'm gay!" and I handed him back his ring. I couldn't be untrue to myself. There were too many lies already. But I also think it was a form of self-punishment – "I'm going to put myself out there to be beat up" – which is what I thought I deserved. After he left, I told my mom, who thought it was some phase.

I went back to school, my sophomore year, and the drinking took off. The only thing that kept me in school was playing sports and singing in choir. But I had to work hard, and I was constantly defending myself. Meanwhile, I was starting to drink a lot more and use meth a lot more. My brother was using, and he and I used a couple of times together. He had been in multiple rehabs; his first trip to jail he was 18 and his first trip to prison was at 23.

Meth gave me the most amazing, false sense of control in the world. I was Wonder Woman and She-Ra all rolled into one. I could walk down a dark alley at two in the morning and not be afraid. Meth was my love, my number one love. By 15, I was selling, here and there, to keep me in drugs. By the time I was 16, I was on the streets a lot exchanging sex for drugs. Eventually, I wound up in the psych unit and for the next several years I was in and out of rehab and in and out of psych units. I was a wreck. I was basically following in my brother's footsteps. He and I were so close, it was almost like we were the same person.

In my junior year of high school, I dropped out, which is one big regret in my life. Between my junior and senior year my choir had a trip planned to go to Europe to sing in the cathedrals. I was the only student who had raised enough money so that I could go, my trip was fully paid for. So, when I dropped out I actually donated all that money to my best friend so that she could go. We're still friends to this day.

I mainly dropped out due to my coming out as a lesbian and I just couldn't continue to tolerate the negativity. My sexual orientation was also one of the main reasons for going in and out of psych hospitals. I would end up be being diagnosed with bipolar and borderline personality disorder as well as dissociative disorder due to the trauma. I became a cutter before anyone really knew what it was and I flipped between bulimia and anorexia because of my control issues. I was on a lot of medication. Mainly anti-psychotics and mood stabilizers. But I wanted to drink so I stopped using some of the meds. The interesting thing is that while I was in the psych hospital I found out I could help people. Nights were terrible for me, but I found worth in helping others. I was very generous, kind and compassionate to everyone but me.

During this time my stepmother and I became very close. She would take me to the beach at times to just get away from my parents' fighting and putting me in the middle. When I was 18 I lived with my dad and stepmother for a time but mainly I was sleeping under bridges and I padlocked myself to my motorcycle at night when I went to sleep because it was my only worldly possession. If you were going to take my bike, you were going to have to take me. I got full-blown into my addiction. My addiction ran from about age 12 to almost age 24.

I got myself into rehab at age 17 the first time after I had intentionally overdosed on meth to try to kill myself. I went into rehab and then fell in love with one of the female counselors which was a cycle I repeated several times over. Just like my brother, at age 18 I wound up in jail. I was arrested for possession and was let out on my own recognizance. About this time, I got into my first serious adult relationship with another woman. We met at a 12-step group for homosexuals. She was 15 years older than me and I reintroduced her to meth after she had been clean for 16 years and she became my dealer. She bought me a van when my motorcycle got taken by a dealer. I couldn't keep a job even though I kept getting jobs. And this went on for years.

After my first arrest there was a second. My arrests were 30 days, 60 days, 90 days, and then finally the judge gave me 18 months in the state penitentiary. My brother was in and out of jail and at the age of 23 he was in prison. I spent my 23rd birthday waiting to go up to prison from the county jail. Which was ironic because the last arrest was the only time that I really hadn't done anything.

Being in the state pen was very humbling. Having to come to terms with my house being raided, the woman I was living with, who was a normy, not wanting anything to do with me. But I excelled! I liked it! I could have done it for the rest of my life with my eyes closed. It was my vacation from my insanity. The problem was I had never been locked up long enough. So, this time, I shed all my defenses. They didn't have enough beds so five of us wound up in administrative segregation. The jail within the prison. The first morning I woke up and I peeked out of the peephole. And I hear a voice. "What?" I think, I'm losing my mind. And then I realize that the voice is coming through a vent. And the voice says, "What's going on?" And I was watching women walking around, doors open, doing laundry behind a chain-linked fence and I asked, "What's that down there?" And the voice says "Oh. That's death row." Now I'm thinking, "How did I get here?"

When I was in jail waiting to go up to prison, one of the inmates asked me, "So. When we get up to the yard, what are you going to be?" "What do you mean?" "What are you gonna be?" I responded, "An inmate?" She says, "Nah. Nah, fool! What're you going to be?" I respond, "A number?" I'm thinking of all the things you are in prison. She goes, "No! Are you going to be a butch or a stud?" "Oh!" I said, "I think I'll just be me!" I think that was a pivotal moment when I made that statement – "I think I'll just be me." I realized at that moment I did not want to be all these masks. All these different things I was pretending to be.

I had over six months clean at that point and I just thought, "I am done!" I did my time next to murderers, but the difference was I was going home, and they weren't. All during the time I was in and out of jail the guards would say, "You don't belong here," or the inmates would say, "What are you doing here, you don't belong here!" and I wound up thinking, "Good God, where do I belong?"

I got out of prison. Stayed clean, though I did relapse once. I came home after interviewing for a new job and found a girl, with my brother, on the couch smoking a pipe. So, I took a hit and then I get a call from the job, asking if I could in for a drug test within 24 hours. Then my best friend called, and I told her what was happening. I ended up going with her and my future wife to the aquarium for the day instead of staying in the house and getting loaded.

After the aquarium I went back to my friend's house. I got a call from my mom saying that my brother was being sent back to prison for driving a stolen van and being high on meth. When I heard that I hit my knees. I knew that could have been me. But I was tired of going to jail and, hey, I already knew I didn't fit in there! So, I didn't go back. I went to college instead. It was rough because I didn't even have a high school diploma, so while in Community College I also went to Adult School and completed my High School Diploma. I graduated from community college with my AA degree with Honors and eventually I got my BS in Psychology.

Later on, my brother was once again out of prison and he borrowed my mom's car, only he didn't show up the next day. My brother had been in a car accident and he was in the hospital on life support. And we had to have the machines turned off three days later. All my brother's friends showed up – big, burly, dudes – falling in my arms, crying. Now my family is more afraid that I'm going to get in a car accident and die at age 28 like my brother. The irony is that I did get in a car accident at age 28. Had I been still using meth, my mom would have lost both of us. I truly believe with all my heart that he died to save my life. He showed me what would have happened to me if I kept on going down that road. He told my mom once, "I won't live to see 30," and he didn't.

The sad thing is that now my other brother is a full-blown opiate addict and is fully supported by my mother. He holds her hostage emotionally; she doesn't want to lose another son. I don't blame her. I'm very angry at him. As for me, I've been clean 20 years. I'm married and have a stepson that I have helped raise since he was 7. Schooling became my recovery. My addiction is just a piece of everything. I've learned so much over the years. Now I am a certified addiction specialist, life coach, instructor for a training institute for addiction counselors, and recently began getting back into public speaking.

## Questions for Discussion

1. The text reveals that most research on family therapy and addiction treatment has been done with adolescents. What do you think accounts for this? BFST holds that the person who is motivated and is in a position of influence to change is the best person to work with in therapy. How might this be applied to research on adults and addiction treatment?
2. BFST distinguishes between the pseudo-self and the solid self. What are the differences between these two? How would someone know if they are operating from either position?
3. Emotional triangles are a key concept in BFST. What makes this so important? What is the best response once an active triangle has been identified?
4. Step 4 of the 12 steps requires a "searching and fearless moral inventory." What do you think is the intention of this exercise?

# 7

# IMPLEMENTATION IN CLINICAL PRACTICE

> We can comprehend every single life phenomenon, as if the past, the present, and the future together with a superordinate, guiding idea were present in it in traces.
>
> Alfred Adler

Although the Family Matters Program is an online program, its organizing philosophy ideas can inform individual clinical practice in working with families struggling with an SUD. This chapter offers some suggestions and guidelines for implementation into clinical work.

Psychotherapy is a practice that relies on the knowledge and skills of the psychotherapist. Experienced practitioners as well as those just beginning their training should be committed to and, more importantly, interested in continuing to learn about their ever-evolving field. As a professor in a graduate psychology program, I have observed that those students with the most enthusiasm for the field, who demonstrate a lively curiosity, make the best psychotherapists. These students also exhibit an ability to think about psychotherapy from a philosophical perspective that allows for the client and their presenting problem to be placed into a larger context.

One of my goals in working with graduate students in Marriage and Family Therapy is to assist them in finding a theoretical foundation. I do not expect them to fully settle on one until they complete their licensure process but hopefully when they graduate they have found a perspective that allows them to conceptualize a case and create a treatment plan that is in keeping with their theory. However, as I consistently remind my students, a theory is not a technique. It is a philosophy of change. Thus, one can have a theoretical perspective while also utilizing techniques from other approaches.

For example, a clinician can work from a cognitive-behavioral approach and use a genogram to assess patterns within the family system to help to identify core beliefs and schemas. Similarly, a CBT therapist could use the Gestalt technique of the empty chair to assist clients in identifying automatic thoughts. The clinician is not changing their foundational theory of psychotherapy but using techniques from other approaches. This integration of theory and techniques underscores the ideas presented in this chapter.

## Working with a Family Member of an Individual with Substance Use Disorder

In my work as a clinician in private practice, I have never ceased to be amazed at how often clients do not report addiction or alcoholism as a problem in their relationships. This phenomenon has been noted by researchers on family therapy and addiction. As Szapocznik et al. (2003) observed, part of the challenge is related to the family members' tendency to see the problem in the addict and thus, they believe the family member with the addiction is the only one who should be in treatment (p. 43). As the authors explain, "the families who most need counseling are those families whose patterns and habit interfere with their ability to get help for themselves" (p. 43). Treatment resistance is related to the family's inability to adapt effectively to the situation and to collaborate to seek help. Given the propensity to deny and minimize in families of addicts and alcoholics, a clinician can expect to discover that addiction or alcoholism is contributing to many of the issues clients even if they do not report this initially.

## A Case Example

The following is an illustration of how the Family Matters Program can be integrated into clinical practice. This case is one that is based on several I have worked with in the past. Identifying characteristics have been changed.

*Olivia and her husband, John, a couple in their mid-fifties, came in for marital therapy. During our first session it was apparent that John was uncomfortable, and he frequently stated that he believed that Olivia was making a bigger deal out of their marital issues than was warranted. One issue that Olivia was concerned about was her husband's insomnia. When I asked what was so troubling about this, she responded that she didn't know what he was doing when he got up in the night. "He just sits there in the dark" she explained. He responded that he had insomnia and that it wasn't that big a problem. I was confused about her emotional response, but further questioning did not result in clarification.*

*Eventually, John seemed to become more comfortable in attending sessions, though he still complained that they only exacerbated their problems and made things worse. John did, however, believe that overall their marriage had improved. Olivia, on the other hand, continued to experience distress. She reported that she had spent most of their 20-year marriage smoothing things over when John got upset and was getting tired of trying to prove that she was a good wife. She finally disclosed that she was concerned about his drinking. He refuted that this was a problem and countered with accusing her of trying to run his life.*

*This stalemate continued until, during one session, John became so agitated in the session that he accused Olivia of being crazy and stormed out of the office. He eventually returned, somewhat calmer, and I suggested that they come in separately for the next session as it was difficult for them to maintain emotional equilibrium when they were together. During an individual session, Olivia disclosed that she was concerned that John frequently drank an entire bottle of wine in order to go to sleep at night. She reported that she also thought he drank too much when he had his friends over and she was not at home.*

## Discussion

Working with family members, as with working with an addict or an alcoholic, means that you will encounter a high degree minimization and denial. While Olivia presented the problem as insomnia and John's staying up late, her real concern was his level of drinking. As the addict/alcoholic, John can be expected to deny his addiction but, as research has shown, family members are equally likely to deny the impact addiction has on them and their family. This was demonstrated in my work with John and Olivia.

### *Begin by Identifying Family Patterns and Individual Core Values*

I began my work with John and Olivia with the treatment goal of teaching them a different way of thinking about the presenting problem and, more importantly, their influence in the family system. I began by constructing a family diagram. A family diagram provides an excellent assessment for identifying relational dynamics and patterns throughout the generations. Identifying patterns assists the client in many ways, primarily by allowing them to step back and take the role of an observer, and at the same time helping the clinician determine some of the client's default attitudes and behaviors. Does this client's family system move toward emotional fusion under stress? If so, the client is likely to respond to a loved one's addiction with an anxious focus and by overfunctioning. Conversely, if the family system tends toward emotional distance, then the client may prefer to sever communication ties, possibly using the excuse of "tough love," to lower his anxiety about his addicted loved one.

Once the family diagram is constructed, the next step is to identify the active emotional triangles. Usually one partner's anxiety about the safety of their loved one will cause him or her to overfunction in a way that perpetuates the addiction. This is called "enabling" in the recovery community. It is an unconscious response in the hope that the loved one will eventually get into treatment. In the case of John and Olivia, Olivia overfunctioned with regard to family relationships. The active triangle was John, Olivia, and their teenage son, Nicholas. John complained that Olivia was overly involved in Nicholas's life while Olivia expressed concern that John didn't spend enough time with their son. For both individuals, this was an unconscious mechanism for avoiding the discussion of the most important issue in their marriage.

*The construction of John's family diagram reflected his tendency to minimize issues as he was very reluctant to fill in the details of the emotional processes in his family. He reported growing up in a typical Midwestern family. His father had been a welder in an auto manufacturing plant and his mom stayed home to care for the children and the household. His father had passed away, and his mother was elderly and living with his older sister in another state. John spoke very highly of his mother and sister but did not offer many details about his upbringing, except to say that he grew up in a rough neighborhood and learned to be street-smart at an early age. His oldest brother lived nearby and John had a strained relationship with him. He felt his brother was judgmental and condescending toward him. He reported that his other brother, who lived in their childhood hometown, was an alcoholic. He explained that while he loved his brother, he could never really trust him.*

*Olivia was more open about discussing her family relationships. She came from a similar working-class background. Her father was a salesman and on the road a lot. Her mother was frequently depressed and addicted to prescription drugs; she was also mercurial and unaffectionate. Olivia noted that she wasn't aware of her mother's addiction when she was growing up but eventually figured this out when she went into psychotherapy in her early 30s. Olivia's only sibling, an older brother, is a recovering alcoholic with 20 years of sobriety. Both of Olivia's parents had died and she had little regular contact with her brother or other family members. She and John met shortly after his divorce and she reports that he "swept her off her feet." Much of her expressed desire in our sessions was to get back to the early days of their marriage.*

## Discussion

It is very common in couples counseling that one of the partners is in greater pain than the other about their relationship. Typically, this person is the overfunctioner with regard to the marriage. This was the case with John and Olivia, with Olivia taking responsibility for maintaining the relationship. Though both the overfunctioner and underfunctioner are in a position to make a change, usually the overfunctioner is in the most pain and is thus more motivated to change. This was apparent in Olivia, as she was highly distressed about their marriage while John remained calm and dismissive.

To change the level of overfunctioning to a level that is in line with a client's principles, it is helpful to assist the client to identify their core values. The goal is to help the client in responding based on their values and principles rather than their feelings. Overfunctioners typically react by going into action as soon as they become anxious. To slow down this process, the client can take a step back and consider the principles or values that might better serve them and the relationship.

Olivia was deeply committed to her Christian faith and this presented her with at least two values that she needed to consider.

1. She valued being a loving wife
2. She valued living in integrity with her religious beliefs

We began by exploring her definition of what it means to be a loving wife. Who determines what is loving? Does she? Does her husband? If her husband is the determinant, does that mean she does everything he tells her to? Would this include illegal activity? If not, then would she be unloving if she didn't do what he wanted?

Clients typically have very vague ideas as to their core values. They have not taken the time to work through the implications of their values or principles because no one has assisted them in this process. This is why values often seem to be competing with each other. This was the case for Olivia. Because of John's lifestyle, her desire to be a good wife seemed to be in conflict with her value of being an exemplary Christian.

### *The Key Question: Am I Investing in Addiction or Am I Investing in Sobriety?*

*John's behavior escalated. He insisted that his wife was flirting with men when they went out and he became angry for what he believed was blatant disrespect. He reported that she was probably not aware of how much she was flirting but he had pointed this out to her repeatedly over the years to no avail. She denied flirting and stated, instead, that she made it a point to avoid eye contact with other men so that her husband would not get upset. John reported that he had put a GPS tracking device on Olivia's car in order to see where she went during the day and had hidden a camera in their bedroom so that he could monitor her activity when he was out of town. Olivia was deeply hurt by this revelation as it represented a tremendous betrayal of trust. She later discovered that he had several sexual encounters with young women during his business trips. His response when she confronted him was to apologize and then insist that they should "move forward" and not let this incident ruin their marriage. When she brought it up in the therapy session, he insisted that he was done with this behavior and that she should just let it go.*

*Things came to a tipping point when John insisted that he had recordings of Olivia having sex with men. She brought this up during a session and demanded that he play one of the recordings. The recording revealed nothing but white noise and static, but John insisted he would hire an expert to "clean" it up and that he could clearly hear her having phone sex on the recording. She responded by tearfully begging him to stop spying on her. He sat and listened stoically while offering no reassurance that he would discontinue his behavior.*

*John came on his own to the next session. I began the session by listing the behaviors that I had observed or that had been reported to me:*

1. *Frequent agitation*
2. *Pressured speech*
3. *Difficulty going to sleep at night*
4. *Use of alcohol to calm himself*
5. *Paranoia*
6. *Hypersexuality*

*I stated that there were two possibilities. One is that he has an organic brain disease which would require a medical evaluation. And the other is that he is using meth or cocaine. I'd hoped it was the latter as this would be simpler to treat. He confirmed that, yes, he had been using cocaine. He agreed to go into treatment the next week.*

*Olivia came in for a session the subsequent week and reported that John was in a treatment facility. She then explained that she had found drug paraphernalia in his closet, but she hadn't known about his use of cocaine; given his behavior over the past year, she was not surprised. She had discovered that large sums of money were missing from their bank account over the years and now understood that this money was going to buy cocaine. She wondered what she should do now that his drug use was out in the open.*

## Discussion

One way to help clients think strategically about responding to a loved one's addiction is to ask whether the action being considered is an investment in addiction or sobriety. An investment in sobriety would require the client to determine what they are willing to support with their time, energy, and finances. The key question is what behaviors go along with addiction versus those that correspond to sobriety. Attending regular 12-step meetings falls into the sobriety category. Being willing to be periodically drug-tested would be another behavior that goes along with sobriety. Helping a loved one with basic needs, i.e., food, shelter, and transportation are more challenging decisions. When does this assistance move from supporting sobriety to enabling continued addiction? The answer is not always easy to determine but the effort to evaluate this and to act with intention is more important than the immediate outcome in changing the family system.

This process can take some time because unless the client is ready to take a position, in other words, hold onto their core value, they will not be able to follow through and remain firm in their decision. The essential question for Olivia was, "What am I willing to live with in my marriage?" Up to this point, Olivia had tolerated infidelity, dishonesty, and verbally aggressive behavior. She had to determine if this toleration was based on her values or her feelings. She admitted she'd been afraid to confront John since he was the breadwinner in the family and she felt financially vulnerable. In addition, she confirmed that she had had her suspicions that he was using drugs but didn't want to believe that this could be true.

*Though John was compliant with treatment, he continued to insist that Olivia was the cause of his drug use. He also stated that he believed 12-step programs were excuses for weak-minded people and he declined to attend meetings. This meant that Olivia would need to determine what her next course of action would be. She wanted to bring her behaviors in line with her values. She knew that she would not be willing to live with John if he did not actively embrace sobriety. She began to attend Al-Anon meetings and gained a great deal of insight and support. What she learned was that John had not really ever taken the first step of admitting he was powerless over his addiction. She also examined her contribution to her current situation – turning a blind eye to his behaviors; covering up for him when he'd been drunk the night before; making excuses for his irritability and hostile verbal behavior.*

*Once John discharged from his program, he returned home stating he was over his cocaine use and would require no aftercare. He was confident he would never use again, and that Olivia and he could get back to the way they were before if she would just be reasonable. Olivia was emphatic that she would not go back to the way things were before, so she decided to move out of the house and find a place to live nearby. She explained that she was not willing to live with someone who had not embraced recovery and she did not trust that he could so easily put his drug use behind him. She did not file for divorce but, instead, became more focused on her own life journey and less on what John was or wasn't doing. This represented a significant change for Olivia as she had centered her life around John for many years.*

When a client takes a firm position, they are likely to feel guilty and anxious. This can often cause them to back down. It is helpful, therefore, to have clients state what they are willing to do, not just what they are not going to do. "I'm not willing to live with you as long as you aren't embracing sobriety, but I am open to having a weekly date night with you," was something that Olivia decided she would say. She knew that there had been other problems over the years that she had ignored. "It's not just the cocaine," she stated, "I can't go back to pretending that we were this great couple when things are really difficult much of the time."

### Taking a Position and the 12-Step Family Groups

As you will recall from our discussion in Chapter 6, taking a position is different from an ultimatum. An ultimatum is other-focused; its goal is to get the other person to change. A position is self-focused, based on principles and values. In addition to regular sessions with a qualified psychotherapist, attending Al-Anon, Nar-Anon, or some other 12-step family group can be invaluable. The philosophy of 12-step family programs encourages members to stay focused on their own lives, and attending meetings regularly, finding a sponsor and working the steps are tremendously helpful in this endeavor. It's not possible to stop focusing on someone you are anxious about unless you can replace this thought pattern with something else.

Much as an addict or alcoholic can achieve lasting sobriety within the program and community of AA, so too can family members learn to find serenity and peace even if their loved one does not become sober. While 12-step meetings do not provide psychotherapy, they are an excellent resource. A good 12-step family group will reinforce the ideas that the client will be discussing in their therapy sessions and assist the client in implementing them in the intervening week. Moreover, a 12-step family group provides peer support and a community that extends beyond that which a psychotherapist can provide.

*Olivia found several regular Al-Anon meetings that were very helpful to her. She attended these weekly and added extra meetings when she was highly anxious. She found a sponsor with whom she developed a good relationship and who could serve as an active support person in her efforts to define herself. Olivia reported that she was learning a lot in the meetings and her therapy sessions revealed that she was much less focused on John than she had been in the past. At one point, she caught herself becoming angry at John for not changing and stated, "I need to stay in my own lane!" She was able to quickly restore self-focus.*

## Discussion

The goal of psychotherapy is lasting change. And while theories differ with regard to how this is best accomplished, assisting clients who have a loved one struggling with addiction or alcoholism will involve creating a strategy for change, implementation of that strategy, and reviewing and refining the client's understandings and insights.

Working from a family systems perspective will assist the clinician and the client in identifying the ways in which the system has contributed to the issue, and the ways in which the client is contributing to the maintenance of the problem. Many clients initially do not understand how changing themselves will help their addicted loved one. It seems counterintuitive, and yet they have also experienced the frustration, powerlessness, and ineffectiveness of trying to get their loved one to change.

Identifying a client's defaults when it comes to challenging interpersonal issues is the first step in this process. Finding out what they have done in the past that was successful is also important. Once this is done, then it is possible to co-construct a strategy that is predicated on a change made by the client. Again, the focus cannot be on the addict or alcoholic. While this may be something that the client agrees with, most likely they will report to you that they "tried" the strategy that that was decided upon in the last session and "it did not work." When asked "How do you know that it didn't work?" usually clients will respond that their loved one didn't do something different. This is a good indicator that the client has not really changed. They are still searching for the magic formula that will get their loved one to stop abusing drugs or alcohol. Therefore, the definition of success has to be something else. Something that is different in the client. This change might include a new perspective that allows him or her to hold a position without being defensive or backing down. Or perhaps the change would be evidenced by a day in which the client was less focused on the addict and experienced a measure of serenity and peace.

*Olivia reported that she was less likely to engage in arguments with John than she had been in the past. At the same time, she was also much more likely to state her views regardless of John's potential reaction. She stopped defending herself when he accused her of flirting. Instead, she explored his thinking by asking questions. This was a difficult task given John's vague responses at times, but she persevered. She also examined how their marriage replicated her relationship with her pill-addicted mother, who would either be cold and withholding or would fly into a rage at the drop of a hat. She could see that she had been responding to John in the same way. This insight helped her to determine strategies for change as she could start with what her typical response would be either with her mother or her husband. She also developed a closer relationship with her brother, who was in recovery for alcoholism and active in the AA program. Finally, she began to explore ways to find an outlet for her creativity, taking a class on art appreciation at a local college and looking into a program to become an art therapist. When I last met with her, Olivia was amazed at how far she had come and was appreciative of the clarity she had achieved.*

## Conclusion

The Family Matters Program focuses on working with family members of alcoholics or addicts to change themselves so that their lives will work better and to create a family system that encourages and supports recovery. This same can be said for work in a traditional clinical setting. The combination of BFST and the program of Alcoholics Anonymous provides clinicians with a road map for deep and lasting change. Instead of working directly with the alcoholic or addict, often the person who is in the least position to make a change, this approach holds that a change in the system will improve their chances for recovery. This is an approach that is uniquely suited to the field of marriage and family therapy and it offers a different way to address the problem of addiction. If one person in a family changes for the better, by definition the family has improved, even if only incrementally. Olivia and clients like her, family members who struggle with their loved one's addiction, can learn to respond to these challenges and grow themselves in the process.

## One Addict's Story

*Living the Promises*

You cannot plow a field by simply turning it over in your mind.
Unknown

I was born up in Alaska. My mom was 21 when she had me. She had already had my older brother and then I have two younger brothers. My dad was a lot older than my mom and he was very abusive. My dad used to feed me booze because it was entertainment. I'm not blaming that for my later abuse, but it did predispose me to it. Later on, I found out my dad was schizophrenic and had bipolar disorder, but we didn't know that at the time. My parents were working-class; my dad worked on road construction but in Alaska that was the norm, so we fit right in. My mom ended up leaving my dad and we moved back to where she grew up.

We left Alaska when I was 8 years old. The area we moved into was upper-middle-class for the most part, so it was a big change from where we'd been. My grandparents bought us a house, so we had some place to live but I was wearing homemade clothes to school; I was the only one who was on food stamps at my school and I was really an outcast. But I met some other outcasts and when I was 10 years old I started drinking. When I had my first drink, I actually was able to feel somewhat at ease; drinking made me just stop caring. Prior to that I'd had a couple of suicide attempts; one time I tried to hang myself from a beam in my mom's house so in a weird way, I think alcohol enabled me to not kill myself. All of my friends' parents had alcohol or weed in the house and we knew they wouldn't miss it if we took some. Soon my drinking went from a monthly occurrence, and then a bi-weekly and then weekly. At age 12 I did pot. At age 13 I did my first hard drugs – acid and cocaine. By 14 I had a needle in my arm using cocaine. There was nothing that came across my path that I wouldn't try. I never had any second thoughts. My thought was that if alcohol did that for me, these other drugs would be even better.

In the year when I was 14 a lot happened. Even though alcohol was my main thing, I did cocaine. Sometimes I put down the needle for some time, but my consumption of alcohol was through the roof. My average was about two-fifths of whiskey a night, five nights a week. My initial reason for drinking was "F*** you, Dad!" But before long, it became a part of my lifestyle and identity. I had even had court-ordered AA, but I figured out pretty quickly that I could sign my own attendance cards.

The crazy thing about my story has to do with the fact that I'm part Jewish, even though I wasn't raised in that tradition. The only people who drank the way I did and had the drugs that I wanted were Neo-Nazis. So, I became a part of that group. It was a kind of a self-hatred. It was just adding another thing to what I had always experienced – fear of reality, self-loathing, hating myself more than anything – which made me a good Nazi being a Jew! But I wanted this drug-filled, booze-filled, violence-filled lifestyle. Getting into fights was easier than being emotional.

That same year I got popped for petty possession, but they looked at my school grades and I got put on probation. For some reason I always excelled in school, particularly in math and science. I never did any homework but even while I'd be sleeping through class somehow, I would absorb it. Every single teacher told me I had so much potential; it was such a waste! But being accepted into a group, even though it was the dirtbag group, was more important to me. This went on all through high school. The cops would come to my classroom and say, "Would you come with us?", and that fed into the persona even more. I fully got into the shaved head look and basically f*** you.

My mom had her hands full and when my older brother went off to the army that meant more freedom for me. I would just disappear. I got brought home by the police dozens of times. But somehow, I got through high school. How I graduated is a true mystery. There was a mound of beer cans by the bush where I used to stand and wait for the school bus. That was my norm. I'd be drunk all week at school and then get spun out on the weekends and do what I needed to do for school.

Toward the end of high school, I decided to enlist in the Marine Corps. I did really well in high school and I was planning to be a firefighter but I'm my own worst enemy. The Marine Corps was my backup plan. I got sworn in on my 18th birthday and I was to ship out 11 days later, but I was in jail eight days later. I got arrested for gang affiliation, brandishing a firearm, and being drunk in public. So that put a hiccup in everything. The Marines said, "Get it quashed and we'll take you back." So, I get in front of the judge and my recruiting officer comes in and says "We're wanting to take him. What can we do?" So, the judge agreed to it. So, what do I do? I go out that night and party, except two or three men drinking is not a party. I got charged with discharging a firearm in a residential area, and drunk in public. The Marines couldn't take me now because of the felonies and now I'm really depressed.

I got a job at a drugstore, working just enough. I had all sorts of barters going on; the manager liked me because I could get him cocaine and he'd let me walk out the back of the drugstore with boxes of booze or cartons of cigarettes. And even though I was drunk every day at work, somehow or another, I'd still win all the secret shopper awards! But that was my personality when I was drinking. I'd either be the greatest guy to be around or you better run for your life! It was those two options.

One time, probation came to the house for a checkup and I'd had a normal night of drinking the night before. I still smelled like booze, so they said, "Alright. Get to office before we close." And I was told I got dropped off around midnight and I was just as coherent as I am now, but I blew a .22, 18 hours after I'd been drinking! People were freaking out at the time! My highest was .68! That's the kind of tolerance I had. So then I'm back in jail. But jail was never an issue for me because it was more like a family reunion. I'd see people there from high school or people I knew from before. I'd gone back and forth from jail five or six times at that point.

Finally, something happened that put me on a different path. It started when the police came to my house and dragged me out of bed in front of my baby brother who had his struggles with heroin and this is probably the third or fourth time he'd seen me dragged out of bed with my boxers on, fighting the whole way down. He's bawling his eyes out. But it didn't stop me. Once I got to jail, I started to plan my hustle which meant get people's pills, get the jailhouse wine but this time, because I wasn't drunk when they arrested me, they transferred me over to the workers' dorm. They strip-searched everyone, so I couldn't take anything. We worked in the area where people are already committed to jail time and are in total segregation. We'd do the cleaning, take food over to the inmates, and it was a great way to pass the time; it really was. But this time, I believe it was Christmas Eve or Christmas Day, my family shows up. My mom came, with my half-sister, and some other family members to tell me that my dad had died. And I didn't really care – no emotion about him dying. He wasn't a father to me. Just seeing my mom completely repulsed by my situation, by me; seeing that I didn't have a care in the world and how comfortable I was in jail, gave her the confirmation that was going to be my life. But my dad died alone, unloved and an alcoholic. And now I'm thinking that even though I'm 45 years younger than he was I was doing the exact same thing. I was an alcoholic with no friends and a family who were only there out of obligation.

I had been one of those a**hole atheists who would debate with people who were devout but that night I hit my knees and prayed to something that I had never known. I prayed that I didn't want my dad's story to be my own story; I got the butterfly feeling, I'll admit it. Once I got out of jail, I had a head start with four months sober, I started going to a local AA meeting near my work at a restaurant. I worked the graveyard shift figuring that would keep me busy. That AA meeting at first felt a lot like my usual situation; there were a lot of people with money there so once again, I'm this poor white kid from Alaska, and I felt I did not belong there whatsoever! I started separating myself because I just couldn't relate until one time I heard someone share that they started drinking because they just didn't feel comfortable in their own skin and I thought, "Holy crap! That's me!!" I was fortunate in that I heard the perfect share.

I stuck with that meeting for years and attended four to eight meetings a week. I wasn't drinking or using drugs, but my mental state didn't change; the Big Book mentions "If you sober up a horse thief, you still have a horse thief" which meant I still got into a lot of fights. Every time I got in a fight, it was a parole violation which gets exponentially longer each time. At one point, I had gotten into a fight and was taken to jail. Instead of doing more probation, I opted to take the remainder of my prison sentence and ended up in a state prison. Jail and prison are a lot different! The irony is that when I was drinking and using, I went to jail a whole lot; when I got sober, I went to prison a whole lot. The thing with prison is you get placed into a level of yard depending on a point value. Levels 1 and 2 are easy; and 3 and 4 are really hard and at this point I'm in level 3 with lifers. Somehow, I got through the 8-month sentence and when I got out I was hired back at my restaurant job and then I got a construction job. I was working 50–60 hours a week in construction and weekends at the restaurant just trying to stay busy. Eventually I got an apartment and started doing all this adult stuff. But I got arrested again and went to another state prison. I turned 21 in prison. But I still believed I was able to do whatever I wanted. So, 3 years and 2 months sober, I get into a high-speed chase with the police. I figured if drinking and drugging don't kill me, nothing will. A lot of my stuff while drinking was a train wreck, but early sobriety had even more potential of a train wreck and I let it go that way so many times. I did four months at another state prison. And that was, thank God, the last time I was in prison.

The good news is what my life is like now. Initially, I was doing the program, but I was fighting it. I would never do a thorough inventory. I would never commit myself to it. A lot of my early sobriety was a combination of white-knuckling it and the bare minimum. But around four years of sobriety, I actually started sponsoring one of my own friends from high school. It turns out his dad had multiple decades in the program, and I knew him, but I hadn't made the connection. I'd seen my friend make attempts at meetings before, but this time I had the wonderful opportunity to start sponsoring him at five days sober. I got reacquainted with another high school buddy who has been in the program a couple of months longer than I have and that's when the fun in the program really began. So many of the promises were coming true; that's when a real fellowship started. I actually started living – I was able to live as a sober person. We're getting involved and doing things for others; and we're involved in each other's lives. I just recently switched sponsors; I loved my first sponsor, but my new sponsor has taught me a wonderful way of approaching the program with simplicity and thoroughness.

Now I'm the guy in my family that when they go out of town, they give me the keys to their house. I've been the best man at multiple friends' weddings. I went from my inevitable future of alone, drunk and then, dead, to this! I started at the construction company right out of prison and I'm now the lead foreman. I've generated so much money for my company that I'm getting a really big bonus at the end of the year. The best thing is that the owner of the company has become a mentor. He's the kind of boss every boss should be. He encouraged me to learn welding and when business was slow, he suggested I try blacksmithing. I ended up putting some of my work into an art exhibition. I'm in line to be a co-owner with another top guy. But the most amazing thing is that the owner of the company introduced me at meetings as his son! To go from the dad I had to this is just incredible. Going from being the person that people were repulsed by, being randomly searched all the time, to what I have now it's all from the program and from sobriety. These are the tangible benefits. Those intangible things – the love and the trust – that's the proof that what I'm doing is working. And it's getting better all the time. I'm 13½ years clean and sober; I have a great job and a future; I'm married. I have a rich, full life.

## Questions for Discussion

1. This chapter presents some ways in which the ideas informing the Family Matters program can be implemented in a clinical setting. How do you see yourself applying these ideas in the future? Which might be the easiest? Which do you think would be the most difficult?
2. The case of John and Olivia is presented as an example. What are your thoughts about the way in which John's addiction was revealed? Why do you think that Olivia did not present this issue at one of their first sessions?
3. Discuss the idea of taking a position and how this was applied in Olivia's case. What was her position about John's addiction? What do you think about her options? What do you think John's response might have been?
4. One of the underlying principles from BFST is the idea that one motivated individual of influence can change a family system. How was this demonstrated in the case of John and Olivia? Who was the motivated person? What makes someone motivated?

# CONCLUSION

> The sway of alcohol over mankind is unquestionably due to its power to stimulate the mystical faculties of human nature.
>
> William James

Navigating the stormy waters of addiction is challenging not only for addicts and alcoholics but particularly for those who love them. One might argue that in some ways, the suffering of family members is greater than that of their addicted loved one. It is a testament to this that one of the founding fathers of the United States, Dr. Benjamin Rush, had a lifelong interest in treating alcoholism, having been raised by an alcoholic father. And yet for the most part families struggling with addiction have been either vilified as the cause, ignored as inconsequential, or told that their actions or inactions are making matters worse. While most treatment programs offer a family program of some sort, what SAMSHA terms "family involved therapy," family therapy in which the family is the focus of treatment, has not been implemented

(Center for Substance Abuse Treatment, 2004, p. 16, known as TIP39). As the authors observe, "Incorporating family therapy into substance abuse treatment presents an opportunity to improve the status quo" (p. 24).

But changing the status quo can be a daunting task, particularly in a culture that is so wedded to a linear, cause-and-effect mindset and a denial of the significance of the family once one has entered adulthood. The fact remains, however, that current modes of treatment must incorporate family therapy if treatment outcomes are to improve. Conversely, acceptance of the status quo means that addicts, alcoholics, and their families must settle for multiple treatment episodes and wasted years of life spent in cycles of use, treatment, and relapse. And this cycle describes only those fortunate enough to survive the immense risk of relapse. While efforts by the medical community to find a cure may someday come to fruition, family therapy is available now.

The barriers to integration of family therapy in substance abuse treatment are twofold: 1. the need to provide mental health professionals trained in family therapy and 2. the reluctance of insurance companies to reimburse for family therapy. Current models of substance abuse treatment rely heavily on chemical addiction counselors to provide counseling and psychoeducation. While these individuals are trained and certified within their scope of practice, they are not qualified to provide family therapy. This would require licensed mental health professionals who are trained in family therapy. Though this would increase the cost of treatment, as the TIP39 authors note, "the documented cost savings and public health benefits associated with family therapy support the idea of reimbursement" (Center for Substance Abuse Treatment, 2004, p. 25).

In addition, to the cost of providing family therapy, the second obstacle lies in the reluctance of insurance companies to pay for family therapy. As the authors further explain, "the American health care insurance system focuses care on the individual. Little, if any, reimbursement is available for the treatment of family members" (Center for Substance Abuse Treatment, 2004, p. 25). In other words, insurance companies would rather pay for multiple treatment episodes than reimburse for family therapy.

One reason for this is the lack of research on family therapy in general and substance abuse treatment and family therapy in particular. The research that exists tends to focus on family therapy and adolescent drug abuse treatment. This highlights a deeply held belief in our society that families are inconsequential to current adult experience. The therapy manual on Brief Strategic Family Therapy for Adolescent Drug Abuse published by the NIDA states, "BSFT has not been tested with adult addicts. For this reason, BSFT is not considered a treatment for adult addiction" (Szapocznik et al., 2003, p. 3). This statement underscores the assumption that family importance ends once an individual enters adulthood. It also leads to the question "Why has BSFT not been tested on adult addicts?"

Similarly, a publication by SAMSHA entitled *Family therapy can help: For people in recovery from mental illness or addiction* states, "Family therapy tends to be most helpful once the person in treatment is fully committed to the recovery process and is ready to make more changes" (p. 5). It goes on further to explain that this might be after a year or more of recovery. There are no references to research that supports this contention, which has been a truism in the field of addiction treatment for years. Given that the likelihood of an individual achieving one year or more of sobriety is low, and the fact that family therapy has never been a part of substance abuse treatment for adults, and rarely for adolescents, it would seem that there is a striking need to change these assumptions.

As we have seen, treatment of addictions and alcoholism has not changed substantially since the first treatment program was established in the United States in 1864. As a society, we have been chasing the goal of recovery from substance abuse for over 150 years with the focus on the individual and little to no consideration of the family system.

Moreover, unlike other family therapies, a family systems approach does not require every member to participate. According to BFST, what is required is one motivated individual who is, or would like to be, influential in the family to begin the process of change. What is needed now is a consistent implementation of this approach into substance abuse treatment. This would provide the necessary conditions for the collection of empirical data to support making family therapy an integral part of substance abuse treatment programs.

What we do know is that family systems therapy will improve the lives of the family members of addicts and alcoholics. What we hypothesize is that an improvement in family functioning will also result in better outcomes for substance abuse treatment and create the necessary relational and emotional environment to support lasting recovery. This book, and the Family Matters Program, was written with this goal in mind. It is now up to the field of psychotherapy in general, and marriage and family therapy in particular, to carry this forward.

# References

Anonymous. *Twelve steps and twelve traditions.* (1981). New York: Alcoholics Anonymous World Services, Inc.

American Psychiatric Association. (2000). *Diagnostic and statistical manual of mental disorder.* 4th ed. Washington, DC: APA.

Becker, H. S. (1953). Becoming a marihuana user. *American Journal of Sociology,* 59(3), 235–242.

Bowen, M. (1986). *Family therapy in clinical practice.* Northvale, NJ: Jason Aronson.

Bowen, M. and Kerr, M. (1988). *Family evaluation: The role of the family as an emotional unit that governs individual behavior and development.* New York: W. W. Norton.

Brown, S. and Lewis, V. (1999). *The alcoholic family in recovery: A developmental model.* New York: The Guilford Press.

Center for Substance Abuse Treatment. (2004). *Substance abuse treatment and family therapy: A Treatment improvement protocol TIP 39.* HHS Publication No. (SMA) 15-4219. Rockville, MD: Substance Abuse and Mental Health Services Administration.

Conyers, B. (2009). *Addict in the family: Stories of loss, hope, and recovery.* Center City, MN: Hazelden Publishing. Kindle Edition.

Cook, L. (2007). Perceived conflict, sibling position, cut-off, and multigenerational transmission in the family of origin of chemically dependent persons: An application of Bowen Family Systems Theory. *Journal of Addictions Nursing,* 18(3), 131–140.

Drake, J. R. (2011). Differentiation of self-inventory-short form: Creation and initial evidence of construct validity. PhD diss., University of Missouri.

Gately, I. (2008). *Drink: A cultural history of alcohol.* New York: Gotham Books.

Gilbert, R. (1992). *Extraordinary relationship: A new way of thinking about human interactions.* Minneapolis, MN: Chronimed Publishing.

Hallstone, M. (2002). Updating Howard Becker's theory of using marijuana for pleasure. *Contemporary Drug Problems,* 29(4), 821–845. Retrieved from https://tcsedsystem.idm.oclc.org/login?url=http://search.proquest.com.tcsedsystem.idm.oclc.org/docview/233173926?accountid=34120

Hanson, R. (2013). *Hardwiring happiness: The new science of contentment, calm and confidence.* New York: Harmony Books.

Hogue, A., Dauber, S., Samuolis, J., and Liddle, H. (2006). Treatment techniques and outcomes in Multidimensional Family Therapy for adolescent behavior problems. *Journal of Family Psychology,* 20(4), 535–543.

Horigian, V., Feaster, D., Brincks, A., Robbins, M., Perez, M., and Szapocznik, J. (2015). The effects of Brief Strategic Family Therapy (BFST) on parent substance use and the association between parent and adolescent substance use. *Addictive Behaviors*, 42(3), 44–50.

Jay, M. (2010). *High society: The central role of mind-altering drugs in history, science and culture.* Rochester, VA: Park Street Press.

Lewis, M. (2015). *The biology of desire: Why addiction is not a disease.* New York: Perseus.

Minuchin, S., Reiter, M., and Borda, C. (2014). *The craft of family therapy: Challenging certainties.* New York: Routledge.

Murdock, N. and Gore, P. (2004). Stress, coping and differentiation of self: A test of Bowen theory. *Contemporary Family Therapy*, 26(3), 319–335.

National Institute on Drug Abuse (NIDA). (2007). *Drugs, brains and behavior: The science of addiction.*National Institutes of Health Publication No. 14-5605. Bethesda, MD: National Institutes of Health.

Rohr, R. (2011). *Breathing under water: Spirituality and the twelve steps.* Cincinnati, OH: Franciscan Media.

SAMSHA. (2013). *Family therapy can help: For people in recovery from mental illness or addiction.* SMA15-4784. Rockville, MD: US Department of Health and Human Services.

Schaub, M., Henderson, C., Peic, I., Tossmann, P., Phan, O., Hendriks, V., Rowe, C., and Henk, R. (2014). Multidimensional family therapy decreases the rate of externalizing behavioral disorder symptoms in cannabis abusing adolescents: Outcomes of the INCANT trial. BMC Psychiatry, 14(1), 26. Doi:10.1186/1471-244x-14-26.

Skowron, E. A. and Friedlander, M. L. (1998). The differentiation of self-inventory: Development and initial validation. *Journal of Counseling Psychology*, 45(3), 235–246.

Standage, T. (2005). *A history of the world in six glasses.* New York: Bloomsbury.

Szapocznik, J., Hervis, O., and Schwartz, S. (2003). Brief strategic family therapy for adolescent drug abuse. *Therapy manuals for drug addiction.* Bethesda, MD: National Institutes of Health.

White, W. (2014). *Slaying the dragon: The history of addiction treatment and recovery in America.* Bloomington, IL: Chestnut Health System.

# INDEX

For Product Safety Concerns and Information please contact our EU representative GPSR@taylorandfrancis.com
Taylor & Francis Verlag GmbH, Kaufingerstraße 24, 80331 München, Germany

www.ingramcontent.com/pod-product-compliance
Ingram Content Group UK Ltd.
Pitfield, Milton Keynes, MK11 3LW, UK
UKHW022201190926
475702UK00003B/143
* 9 7 8 1 1 3 8 7 2 4 7 0 9 *